John Wesley Jaques

Three years' campaign of the Ninth, N. Y. S. M., during the southern rebellion

John Wesley Jaques

Three years' campaign of the Ninth, N. Y. S. M., during the southern rebellion

ISBN/EAN: 9783337207847

Printed in Europe, USA, Canada, Australia, Japan

Cover: Foto ©ninafisch / pixelio.de

More available books at **www.hansebooks.com**

THREE YEARS' CAMPAIGN

OF THE

NINTH, N. Y. S. M.,

DURING THE

SOUTHERN REBELLION

BY

JOHN W. JAQUES,

Formerly of Company D.

NEW YORK.

HILTON & CO., Publishers,
128 Nassau Street.

1865.

Entered according to Act of Congress, in the year 1865, by
JOHN WESLEY JAQUES,
In the Clerks' Office of the District Court of the United States, for
the Southern District of New York.

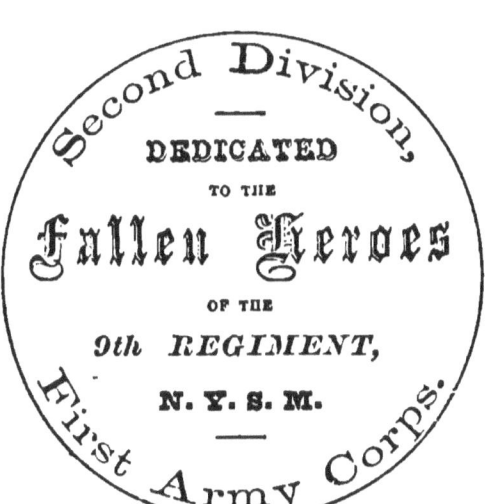

BATTLES

IN WHICH

THE NINTH REGIMENT,

NEW-YORK STATE MILITIA

WERE ENGAGED.

Harpers Ferry, Virginia, July 4, 1861
Cedar Mountain, Virginia, August 9, 1862
Rappahannock Station, Virginia, August 20, 1862
Thoroughfare Gap, Virginia, August 28, 1862
Second Bull Run, Virginia, August 30, 1862
Chantilly, Virginia, September 1, 1862
South Mountain, Maryland, September 14, 1862
Antietam, Maryland, September 17, 1862
First Fredericksburg, Virginia, December 13, 1862
Chancellorsville, Virginia, May 1, 1863
Gettysburg, Pennsylvania, July 1, 1863
Wilderness, Virginia, May 5, 6, and 7, 1864
Laurel Hill, Virginia, May 8, 1864
Spottsylvania, Virginia, May 12, 1864
Coal Harbor, Virginia, June 4, 1865

☞ Besides the four last named battles, there were other, as the regiment was marching and fighting, on their way to Richmond, Virginia, until they left for home, June 8, 1864

PREFACE.

The object of this little book, is to place upon the Annals of History, of the Southern Rebellion, the records of one of those *gallant* regiments, that volunteered their services to put down the traitors. As the Author was a member of the NINTH NEW-YORK STATE MILITIA, he has endeavored to truthfully portray, the marches, incidents, and battles, in which that regiment took an active part, passing through hardships and trials, as true patriots, battling for the cause of their beloved country, and nobly carrying the " Stars and Stripes," to the discomfiture of the rebel hosts. Many of the members of this regiment, gave up their lives on the field of carnage and strife to whose memory, we drop a tear, hoping that our courteous readers, who are endowed with the senti-

PREFACE.

ments of Freedom and Constitutional Liberty, on the perusal of this work, will ever bear in their memory, the hardships and privations, endured by this band of true and loyal patriots, who fought and bled, to preserve the Constitutional Rights of their beloved country.

Many of the regiments have received credit and honor, from the hands of Public Opinion, but shame to tell, a regiment which courageously carried the Banner of its Country, through the campaigns of Virginia and Maryland, for three years ,giving up the lives of many of their comrades, on the field of action, were scarcely or ever noticed, by the scrutinizing hands of Public Opinion, but the Author believes, that these men, who nobly fought for their country, and many who died in its defence, receives a silent and grateful acknowledgement, from a true and loyal people; and that the NINTH REGIMENT, NEW-YORK STATE MILITIA, will ever be remembered by the loyal people of the United States, for the aid it rendered in subduing the Southern Rebellion.

THREE YEARS' CAMPAIGN OF THE "NINTH N. Y. S. M."

CHAPTER I.

From May 27, to August 17, 1861.

THE Ninth New York State Militia, were organized in June 1859, in the city of New York, as a Militia regiment, and received their charter from the state of New York, and elected Michael M. Van Beuren as Colonel, it then consisted of four companies, but at the breaking out of the Southern Rebellion in 1861, there were four more added to the regiment, making it eight companies; their fatigue uniform were dark blue pants with red stripes; jackets with red trimmings on the cuffs; low caps with gilt braid around them, with the letter of the company on the peak; overcoats dark blue, cuffs trimmed with red,and broad capes lined with red.

President Lincoln having issued a call for volunteers to put down the Southern Rebellion, after the rebels had fired upon Fort Sumpter in Charleston Harbor, April 1861; the Ninth responded to the call, and commenced recruiting to fill up their ranks, which having done in a few weeks, they tendered their services to the War Department at Washington, D. C., but it being too late to be accepted for three months, they offered their services to the "Union Defence Committee," a body of loyal and true citizens, united together to furnish means and transportation to send regiments from New York city to Washington, the seat of war; the committee accepted the regiment, and furnished them with knapsacks, blankets, equipments and clothing, and the men having been sufficiently drilled for active service, after the election by the Board of Officers of a Colonel to command the regiment in place of Colonel Van Beuren, as he found it impossible to go with the regiment, as there were sickness in his family; John W. Stiles ex-Colonel of the "Eighth New York State Militia," was elected to fill the position of Colonel, and all the arrangements being made and the regiment reaching the mimimum number on the afternoon of

Monday, May 27, the regiment marched down Broadway with their blankets strapped on their knapsacks, and overcoats rolled thereon, in their fatigue uniform, with their equipments, (but no arms,) on their way to Washington, to lend their aid and assistance as a band of freemen, to suppress the rebellion, which had sprung up in the southern part of our glorious country, the rebels endeavoring in their madness, to lower that noble old flag—the " stars and stripes under which they were born, and their ancestors had fought and bled to sustain ; all along the route the regiment were received with boisterous cheerings, many a silent prayer were offered up that their dear loved ones would be spared to return home again, to their families and friends, after serving their country faithfully, and rooting out the seeds of the rebellion. That noble old flag waved from many a building, and there was not a downcast countenance to be found in the ranks of these noble patriots, whose thoughts were fixed upon the destiny of their beloved country. Many a young lady's heart beat with joy and pride, as she beheld her *gallant* lover in his splendid uniform, ready to fight the battles of his country. Many a mother as she wiped the tears from her eyes, was proud to see her son in the ranks, willing to serve his country againt traitors, and to protect his home against the ruthless foe. Many a wife offered up a silent "God bless you," as she beheld her husband numbered with this band of true and loyal patriots; and friends shook hands with their friends on parting, with the solemn injunction, "Be true to your country," "fight earnestly in the cause of Freedom and Constitutional Liberty," and "if you live to return home, you will be honored and respected," but, "if you should be killed, it will be in defence of your country, and your name will be handed down to future posterity, as your country, *saviours*

The regiment crossed the Ferry at Courtlandt street, North River, and landed in Jersey City, and that evening took the cars for Washington, D. C., all along the route we were loudly cheered, the "Stars snd Stripes" floated exultingly to the breeze, and cheer after cheer being given for that dear "old flag"; the train in the vicinity of Burlington, N. J., meeting with some impediment, was delayed for some time, when a sad calamity happened to a member of company D.,———, while standing on the bank of the canal, a pistol was accidentally discharged, the ball entering his body and precipitating him into the canal; private Charles Gesner of company D., jumped to his rescue, he recovered the body, but life was extinct; the corpse was sent home to his friends, under the charge of private Charles Gesner.

The regiment crossed the Ferry at Camden.N. J., and landed in Philadelphia, Pa., near the Navy Yard, about day-light

Tuesday 28th., and walked to the Baltimore Depot,taking the cars from there,and going slowly along the road, arrived in Baltimore, Md., about mid-day, expecting to meet there the " Eighth New York, volunteers," who having their *arms* with them, were to escort us through the city, but we were disappointed in not meeting them, so we pursued onr march from the Philadelphia to the Washington Depot, passing through Pratt street, where the " Sixth Massachusetts, volunteers," were attacked by a mob, in April, while on their way to Washington ; but our regiment was not molested, although many a black look was cast upon us,they freely offered us ice-water and other refreshments, but Colonel Stiles had ordered the men not to accept anything from them, as he was afraid they would try to poison us.

We took the cars and before sundown, arrived in Washington city, D. C., and took up our quarters in Woodward's buildings, on Pennsylvania avenue, each company having a room to themselves,and mattrasses filled with straw, to sleep on. The distance from Washington to New York, is 240 miles.

Thursday, 30th.—Marched to the Arsenal

where we were supplied with old Harper's Ferry Muskets, and on

Friday 31st., we marched passed the Presidential Mansion, passing in review before the President and his Cabinet, and also Lieut. General Scott, after which we returned to our quarters in Woodward's buildings.

Saturday, June 1st.—Early in the morning, marched through Pennsylvania Avenue, passing the "Seventh New York State Militia," who were on their way to New York city, having served the thirty days, for which time they were accepted by the Government; we marched out Fourteenth street, and encamped in a field on the Georgetown road, opposite Columbia College, which camp, the "Seventh New York State Militia," had just left. We found the Tents pitched, the "Seventh," having transferred all their camp equipage to the " Ninth"; the appearance of the interior of the tents, showed a liberal supply of mattresses, chairs, wash-basins, etc., having the sign of comfort and ease that that *gallant* regiment must have enjoyed, they also did not forget to leave us some of their preserved meats, and here and there, cordials were found to wash it down with. The Tents were of the style, known as the " Wall Tents," capable of crowding in fourteen persons, and with boarded floors.

Our encampment was named in honor of the then Secretary-of-War,

CAMP CAMERON,

and was finely situated; on the opposite side of the road, was the Columbia College, which was used as an army hospital, and stood on the road leading to Georgetown.

Saturday 8th.—Captain Whipple, U. S. A. visited camp, and the regiment was sworn into the United States service by him, *to serve during the War, unless sooner discharged*, the men being confident of compelling the rebels to return to their allegiance to the United States Government, in a few months. The regiment was about eight hundred and forty strong, when we left New York city, and about forty refused to be sworn in, these were ordered outside of camp, to shift for themselves, and a double guard stationed around it to prevent their return.

While remaining in camp, each company detailed men to do their cooking, when meal-time arrived the men formed in one rank, and were served in their turn, falling out and making room for the next one.

Sunday 9th.—Received orders to be ready for a march, and to take but little clothing, as we expected to return in a week or two, leaving a detail behind in charge of the things that were left.

Monday 10th.—Reveille sounded early, and after breakfast the wagons were packed with our tents and camp equipage, and strapping on our knapsacks, fell into line, and started on our *maiden* march, the day was warm, not a breath of wind stirring, and the road was rough and stony ; the field officers were on foot, they having no horses. During the march the men being greatly fatigued, the wagons carried their knapsacks, and late in the afternoon, passing the " First New Hampshire volunteers," on the road, and encamped on the Fair Ground at ROCKSVILLE, where we pitched our Tents, and detailing a camp guard, and eating our supper, we laid down on the bare ground, with our blankets for a covering, and after a weary and fatiguing march of 18 miles, dropped to sleep.

Tuesday 11th.—We remained encamped all day, on the Fair Ground at ROCKVILLE, which is the county town of Montgomery county, Md., situated on the road leading from Georgetown, in in a north-west direction from Washington ; it is a small town with but few houses in it, the inhabitants were very hospitable and generous towards us ; at sundown a number of ladies and gentlemen visited camp, to see the regiment on Dress Parade, there was also a large assemblage of *contrabands*, who turned up the whites of their eyes, and showed their "ivory's," in astonisment at the movements of the "sojers"; the spectators appeared greatly pleased and gratified at our evolutions, many of them having never seen soldiers before.

One evening after Dress Parade was dismissed, the " First New Hampshire volunteers," who were encamped on the opposite side of the Fair Ground from us, rushed with wild enthusiasm towards us, loudly cheering and throwing up their hats in the air, we shook hands and embraced each other; the feelings that existed between these two regiments, one from New York, and the other from New Hampshire, perfect strangers to each other, but friends in the cause of Freedom, will never be forgotten, and often called to memory, long after the rebellion has ceased; we visited their camp and were cordially entertained by them, their Band played a number of National and patriotic airs, discoursing sweet music to refresh the mind and pass away the *ennui* of camp life; the evening passed pleasantly away, and at *tattoo* we returned to our quarters, with the determination of having a Band of our own, and settling down to rest, we gave up ourselves to the "God *Morpheus*. (sleep.)

Wednesday 12th.—After Breakfast, struck Tents, and took up the line of march, the weather being warm, and the roads in a bad condition; while pursuing our march, a very laughable incident happened, making a subject for conversation, in our after campaign ; it was reported that our wagon train had been attacked by rebel cavalry, the regiment about-faced and marched to the rear, in double-quick time, after marching a little ways, the news was brought that it was nothing but a stampede amongst some horses that had broken out of a field, and run amongst the wagon train, frightening the wagon-master and teamsters, who thought the rebels was in the midst of them ; all becoming quiet, the regiment again, about-faced, and resumed their march, and late in the afternoon passed through the small village of DARNESTOWN, on the outskirts of which, we encamped and pitched our Tents for the night, and after setting the camp guard, retired to rest, after a fatiguing march of 10 miles.

A number of the men visited DARNESTOWN, which is situated near Seneca Creek, in the southeastern part of Montgomery county, Md., and the appearance of the place is very much antiquated with scattering houses here and there ; the inhabitants wer_every hospitable towards us, inviting us to their houses to dine with them, which invitation was accepted by many of our men.

Our camp was situated on the outskirts of the

village, in a large cleared field, skirted by woods and beautiful scenery, with running streams of water, and in a healthy situation. We named the camp in honor of Col. Charles P. Stone, who commanded the " District of Columbia volunteers" and also our regiment.—CAMP STONE.

Visitors came from a long distance, to see the regiment on Dress Parade, and appeared highly gratified and pleased with our evolutions.

Pedlers visited camp with cooked chickens, pies, biscuits, bread, etc., and where largely patronized by the men, which was a change from government rations of hard crackers and bacon.

We remained at camp STONE, about five days, and on the evening of

Monday 17th., it being a splendid moonlight night, we struck our Tents and taking the road to DARNESTOWN, passed through that place and also the small village of DAWSONVILLE, and crossing the bridge over Seneca Creek, encamped for the night, on high ground, near its banks, having marched over good roads, about 4 miles.

Tuesday 18th.—Companies B. and D., left the camp for Sugar Land Bottom, which lays on the Chesapeake and Ohio canal, to do picket duty, about ten miles from camp.

DAWSONVILLE, near which the regiment

encamped, is a small place, with but few houses and very few white inhabitants, but a large number of blacks; it is located in Montgomery county, and is a place of little importance; we remained encamped there till the evening of

Thursday 20th., when we took up our line of march, it being a nice moonlight night, and *bivouac* near POOLESVILLE for the night, having made an easy march of 9 miles.

Friday 21st.—After Breakfast resumed our march, passing through a thinly settled country, the roads were in good condition, but the march was tedious and irksome, the weather very warm; towards sundown we were gladdened with a view of the Potomac river; on ascending a hill, that picturesque and splendid river, for the first time appeared in full view with all of its grandeur and sublimity, the beauties of the surrounding sceneries, elicited many a shout from the admiring spectators; we encamped on a high eminence overlooking the Potomac and Monocacy rivers, near the latter; after posting the camp guard, we retired to rest, having marched 12 miles.

Our encampment we named in honor of Brig. Gen. Hall, commanding the New York State Militia.—CAMP HALL,
it was finely situated, in the vicinity is a large stone aqueduct bridge, spanning the Monocacy;

while remaining encamped here, we picketted about five miles along the Potomac river, doing very heavy duty.

No Major having come from home with the regiment, the officers elected Capt. William Atterbury of company G., to fill that position.

As company E. were picketting along the Potomac, one day, while some of the men were bathing, they heard the report of a musket, and shortly after a shot went whistling by, being the first indication of an enemy ; Capt. Smith immediately crossed over on a small island in the Potomac, with a few men, in an old dug out or scow, but found no one there, looking across the river on the Virginia shore, they espied a small party of men, under the verandah of a house, who politely invited them over to take a hand in " seven up," but the invitation was declined. The house was afterwards burned down, by the order of Brig. Gen. Geary, as it was found to be a *rendezvous* for guerillas.

Dr. Bigelow came from New York, as surgeon of the regiment in place of Dr. Fisher, who remained at home.

Monday, July 1st.—Near sundown leaving our Tents standing, and a detail behind, we marched out of camp, the rain coming down in torrents, the night dark,and the roads muddy and disagreeable ; about midnight we reached the POINT-OF-ROCKS, taking shelter for the remainder of the night, in a large storehouse ; laying ourselves down to sleep if we could, in our wet clothes, after a fatiguing march of 6 miles.

Tuesday 2d.—Left our quarters in the storehouse in the morning, and laid along the Baltimore and Ohio Railroad, where companies B. and D., returned to the regiment from Sugar Land Bottom, where they had been sent the morning after encamping at DAWSONVILLE to do picket duty ; the guard that had been detailed to remain behind with the Tents at the camp, near the mouth of the Monocacy came up ; companies B. and D. was under the command of Capt. Davis of company D., and marching over dirt roads, and through fields, towards evening of the same day, reached SUGAR-LAND BOTTOM, encamping in a fine large apple orchard, where the grass was high, within half-a mile of the Potomac river ; picketted between Edward's Ferry and Seneca Falls a distance of six miles, being ten miles from where they left the regiment.

The rations issued to these companies were scarce and poor, having to forage the country to keep hunger away, and some of the members of company B., making dinner of Frogs as an actual necessity.

One day the pickets hearing the report of musketry in the direction of Seneca Falls, a few men were sent in that direction, nearing the Falls, they found the " First District of Columbia volunteers" engaged with a small party of rebels, and our men went to their support; a sharp firing was kept up about half-an-hour, when the rebels hastily fled to the Virginia shore, the river being about half-a-mile wide at that place; the " District volunteers lost a few men, the loss of the rebels was not known.

Calling in the pickets, companies B. and D., early on the morning of July 1st., marched to rejoin the regiment, at Camp Hall, near the mouth of the Monocacy river, which they reached about sundown, and finding the regiment gone, they remained in camp till the next morning, when they joined the regiment at the Point-of-Rocks, late in the afternoon.

While laying at the Point-of-Rocks, we espied on the Virginia shore, the " Stars and Bars" of Secessiondom, for the first time; it was floating from a flagstaff, where its original claimant, the "Stars and Stripes" formerly floated, but was taken down, to make place for that *dirty rag*; on the abutments of the railroad bridge, (iron) which spans the Potomac, and the rebels had destroyed some time previous, was discovered a rebel battery planted to prevent the Union troops from crossing the river, which is about three quarters of a mile wide at that place.

Wednesday 3d.—Early in the afternoon, companies A. C. and G., under command of the senior officer, Capt. Morrison of company A., took the cars for Sandy Hook, to reconnoitre along the river, and on arriving they took up their quarters in the buildings previously used by Adams' Express Company, as a depot, and in some of the houses ; the distance from the regiment is 8 miles.

Thursday 4th.—The day which one year ago was celebrated throughout the United States, North and South, now witnesses one section of the noble Republic arrayed in conflict against the other, the South with their ruthless hands endeavoring to pull it down, and raise in its stead a yoke more galling than that of Great Britain, previous to the Revolution of 1776.

The day was ushered in by the firing of salutes, and the regiment was drawn up in line, and were addressed by Colonel Stiles, who was loudly applauded ; in the afternoon the regiment marched to Colonel Stones, Head-Quarters, (who was in command of our troops,) and calling for him he made his appearance and addressed us in a short but feeling speech, in which he complimented the " Ninth New York State Militia," we sang a number of National songs, everything passed off pleasantly until the whistling of the Locomotive from Sandy Hook, was heard, which brought tidings that put an end to our enjoyment for the day, as news were brought that the companies which had left the regiment, the day previous on a *reconnoissance*, had been fired upon by rebels secreted behind the abutments of the railroad bridge at HARPER'S FERRY, which some time previous the rebels had destroyed ; our men were exposed to a galling fire, they having nothing to shelter them from rebel musketry. The regiment immediately took the cars to go to their support, on arriving at the scene of action, the fighting was over, the rebels having ceased firing; the river at Harper's Ferry is not more than half a mile wide, and our muskets must have done some execution ; our loss was 1 killed and 2 wounded.

On the morning of the skirmish, some of the men on the reconnoitering party, crossed the Potomac in a small skiff to Harper's Ferry, and went rambling through the town ; they espied a flagstaff, which the U. S. Government had erected years ago, on which were two Flags ; the upper one, the " Stars and Bars," and the lower one, the Virginia State flag, which was blue ; some of the men climbed the flagstaff, to tear down the flags but it being slender and rotten, it was given up in despair by all except private Edwin Butler of company C., who succeeded in carrying away the State's Flag, while some days after, private Nelson Pinard of company H. tore down the other one.

After the skirmish the whole regiment *bivouac* for the night, along the railroad near Sandy Hook and the next morning

Saturday 6th., took up the line of march passing through the principal streets of SHARPSBURG, in which place the glorious " old flag" was seen waving from the principal buildings and houses, and the inhabitants thronged the sidewalks, and the doors and windows of the houses, to have a view of us, and they loudly cheered as we passed through their streets ; halting on the outskirts of the town to cook dinner, the people invited us to dine with them, and insisted upon it, the invitations were accepted, and while we were eating, the young ladies were busy making aprons of *Red, White and Blue*, which they presented to the men after dinner, which we looked upon as a memento of their true and loyal feeling towards the defender's of their country's liberties ; they also presented each company, with a small *Red, White and Blue* Flag ; their motives were entirely patriotic, refusing to receive any compensation, and after heartily thanking them, we resumed our march and after dusk, halted and *bivouac* in the woods on the outskirts of the small village of BAKERSVILLE, after a fatiguing march up hill and down dale, over rough roads on a hot summer's day of 16 miles.

Sunday 7th.—Early in the morning resumed our march, passing through WILLIAMSPORT, near which we forded the Potomac, which is about half a mile wide ; the current runs very strong, and the water is knee deep in most places; some of the men stripped, others took off their shoes and stockings, preparatory to wading the river ; without any accident we put foot on the 'sacred soil" of Virginia about noon, and *bivouac* for the night, near the bank of the river, having marched 7 miles.

While cooking our dinners we perceived the *gallant* "First New Hampshire volunteers" (previously spoken of) fording the river, and halting half way over, their Band played National airs, which were very refreshing to worn out soldiers; after they had crossed the river, they passed us, and continued their march for some distance, when they halted for the night.

Monday 8th.—About noon resumed our march, the weather very warm and sultry, and the roads dusty, passed through a country laid waste by the devastations of an army, marched along the Baltimore and Ohio railroad, and found the rails torn up for a long distance by the rebels ; late in the afternoon passed through MARTINSBURG, where we found Gen. Patterson's Division, who loudly cheered us as we passed ; his troops had driven the rebels from the place, a few days before, who had burned the car buildings, a number of locomotives, a quantity of coal, and a splendid car depot, all of which was the property of the Baltimore and Ohio railroad Company ; they also burned a splendid bridge crossing a small creek near by, but Gen. Patterson's men pressed the rebels so hard, that they could not finish the work of demolition to their cruel satisfaction, so they up with the switches and run a large number of cars into the creek, where they upset. Passed through Martinsburg we bivouac for the night, on a side hill, on the outskirts of the town, in a muddy and disagreeable place, laying with heads up and feet down hill, and fatigued, after marching about 12 miles.

An amusing incident happened to one of the members of the regiment, having received some sausages from home, put them in his knapsack which he used for a pillow, he woke up about midnight, by feeling his pillow moving, and looking up he saw a *porker*, which having scented the sausages was trying to obtain possession of them, but he did not obtain his prize.

Tuesday 7th.—Company K., an Artillery company raised in Rahway, N. J., under the command of Capt. Bunting, and attached to our regiment, joined us while laying here.

Many of the men visited MARTINSBURG, which is the county town of Berkeley county, Va. and before the rebellion, was a thriving place, it contained the work shops and car buildings of the Baltimore and Ohio railroad Company; several miles from town is the splendid and palatial mansion of Robert J. Faulkner, President Buchanan's, Minister to Russia, who turned Traitor to his country, the house was occupied by Maj. Gen. Sandford, who commanded the New York State troops in that vicinity, and by whom we were reviewed.

We made a raid on the poultry and swine that the rebels had left behind them, as a change from government rations of hard bread and salt pork, which were sometimes scarce.

We remained around Martinsburg, about a week, having no shelter to protect us from the weather, except such as we made from the boughs of the trees.

Monday 15th.—In the morning joined Gen. Patterson's Division, which was designated as the "Army of the Upper Potomac," we were assigned to the Brigade of Col. Stone, formerly of the "First District of Columbia volunteers," but recently made Brigadier General, and assigned to the Brigade composed of the First New Hampshire, Seventeenth and Twenty-fifth volunteers, and our regiment; the column marched along till within a few miles of BUNKER HILL, where the infantry halted, and the artillery which had been marching to the rear, double-quicked it to the front, our cavalry had a skirmish with the rebel cavalry, driving them through the town of Bunker Hill, and pursuing them some distance on the Winchester Pike, night coming on our cavalry returned to Bunker Hill, leaving the rebels still retreating ; some of the rebel officers were captured in the town, while partaking of their evening meal, not anticipating danger so near. The column resumed its march, passing through the town, on the outskirts of which, we *bivouac* for the night, in an orchard, being tired and sleepy, after a difficult march of 10 miles.

BUNKER HILL is a small town in Berkeley county, Va., and situated south of Martinsburg the inhabitants are open to trade, supplying us with bread, milk, biscuits, etc., in return for our "greenbacks." There being plenty of blackberries in the vicinity, our men fared sumptuously.

Wednesday 17th.—In the morning taking our position in the column, resumed our march, passing through MIDDLEWAY, taking the road towards Charlestown, after passing Middleway, an amusing incident occurred, which will be spoken of by the members of the "Ninth," as the *Battle of the "Haycocks,"* it was as follows :—

Our cavalry had had a skirmish with a small guerilla party, and the artillery was drawn up in position, and our regiment in line-of-battle, in a field with the hay cut and cocked, loaded our muskets and primed them, and remained on the alert, while Col. Stiles rode up and down the line giving orders (on a horse purchased at Martinsburg,) to be ready for action ; the negro servants of the officers, who left their masters and followed the regiment, took shelter in their fright behind the haycocks, expecting to see "massa Johnson," (Gen. Joseph E. Johnson,) come and take them back to their massa's ; we remained in line-of-battle nearly an hour, when no enemy appearing, we resumed our march, and late in the evening *bivouac* near CHARLESTOWN for the night ; the day was very warm and sultry, and the march tedious, a distance of 8 miles.

The field that we *bivouac* in, was the one that John Brown, the leader of the Harper's Ferry insurrection, was hung in, in the field were two trees, between which stood the gallows, but they had been cut down by *relic-seekers*.

CHARLESTOWN is the county town of Jefferson county, Va., and is a place but of little importance, the male inhabitants are mostly in the Confederate army, while the females remaining at home, are a haughty, scornful set of *she-cessia*, spitting at, and spurning the Union troops, and using such epithets as, "I know what you are after, ' booty and beauty,'" of the former there is but little, while of the latter it is passable ; they also sneeringly asked us, " what we wanted there, why we did not follow ' Johnson,' as he was waiting for us!" to which insults, we turned a deaf ear ; the place was put under martial law and searched, arms and munitions of war, were found secreted in the houses.

Companies B. and E. were detailed to go about three miles from camp, to bring in a number of cars loaded with corn, which the rebels in their hurried flight left behind ; by means of long ropes, company E. drew them along, while company B. guarded them from the rear, with loud shouts and applause from the troops stationed around, they arrived in the town, with the car and its contents.

The Band that we had subscribed for, arrived from home under the leadership of Mr. Neyer, and they were joyfully received by the regiment, the Government also paying them.

Sunday 21st.—Early in the morning took up

up our position in the column, made a slow and easy march, and halted early in the afternoon, on a green knoll, on the side of a hill near BOLIVAR HEIGHTS, not far from Harper's Ferry, where we *bivouac* for the night, having marched 8 miles.

On the Heights commanding the roads at three points, were planted, two thirty-two pounders, with their trunnions knocked off, and the cannons spiked, which had been left by the rebels.

Water was very difficult to obtain, having to go some distance after it.

Monday 22d.—In the morning we again resumed our march, and going about a mile, our orders were countermanded, when we about-faced and marched back to the same place, where we *bivouac* for the night.

In the vicinity is the cave, were John Brown used to secrete himself, some of the men visited the cave, which they found to be long and dark, and with lighted candles explored its interior, in the centre of which they found a spring of water clear as crystal, and cold as ice, which was very refreshing on that warm day of July.

Sunday 28th.—In the afternoon taking up our line of march, re-forded the Potomac at Harper's Ferry, crossing into Maryland, the weather was, showery and windy, the roads dusty, giving us a begrimed appearance, which created laughter amongst us; towards sundown, we *bivouac* for the night on MARYLAND HEIGHTS, near Sandy Hook, after a march of 5 miles.

Monday 29th.—Received our Tents, which we had left at the Point-of-rocks, (July 5th.) having *bivouac* for over three weeks, there being a great deal of rainy and wet weather during the time. We laid out a camp, and named it in honor of Capt. Davis of company D.—CAMP DAVIS, it is situated on a hill on MARYLAND HEIGHTS overlooking Loudon Heights on the Virginia shore, the scenery was really picturesque, at the foot of the hill, was the small village of Sandy Hook, containing a few houses, the Baltimore and Ohio railroad, running through it, and also the Chesapeake and Ohio canal running near the Potomac river, which at that place is very shallow and not more than three quarter of a mile wide. The water for cooking purposes was brought by the teams from the railroad tanks at Sandy Hook, there being only a small spring near camp, that was used for drinking purposes.

Doctor Bigelow bade the men farewell before leaving for home, as he had resigned his position we were sorry to part with him, as he was beloved by the men for his kindness and attention to the sick.

Doctor Howard Pinckney who came from home with the regiment as assistant Surgeon, was the only Doctor left with us.

Besides the usual camp and picket duties, men were detailed to guard the wagon and ammunition train, and also to work on the fortifications on Maryland Heights.

The "First New Hampshire volunteers" term of service having expired, they started for Sandy Hook, to take the cars for home, and our men went down to see them go. We gave them cheer upon cheer, which they returned; they were eager for us to change uniforms with them, we did so, this one, with our jackets, another one, with our overcoats, still others, with our pants and caps, and as they passed through the city of New York, the people must have thought that the "Ninth" were coming.

New recruits for company D. joined their company, having arrived from New York city.

The regiment was very healthy, there having only two deaths occurred which were Typhoid Fever, and both were buried in the vicinity of camp, one of the body's was afterwards taken up and sent home to his friends.

Several times the Tents were struck, ready for a march, but the orders being countermanded the Tents were again pitched.

We received a visit from Major Lawlor, who came to pay off the regiment from the time that we were mustered into the United States service, which was paid in specie.

The want of money had not been badly felt, as Mr. Edward Ralph, jr. our enterprising sutler, gave the men credit for his goods, until they were paid off.

A short time afterwards, received a visit from Major Sherman who came in place of Major Lawlor, to pay the regiment the time between mustering in and enlisting.

From May 27th to August 17th, 1861, the regiment made thirteen marches, travelling 125 miles.

CHAPTER II.

From August 17, to December 4, 1861.

Saturday August 17th.—Early in the morning broke camp, and taking our position in the Brigade, composed of the Twenty-ninth Pennsylvania, Twenty-seventh Indiana, and Third Wisconsin volunteers, which regiments were put in the Brigade, in place of the First New Hampshire, Seventeenth and Twenty-fifth Pennsylvania volunteers, which were three months regiments, their time having expired, they were mustered out of the service; the Brigade was put under command of Brig. Gen. Hamilton, formerly Colonel of the Third Wisconsin volunteers, who relieved Brig. Gen. Stone ; the Brigade pursued its march over rough and bad roads, with small streams running across them, and mud in abundance ; it was a march up and down hills, through woods and valleys, and across fields ; passed through the village of KNOXVILLE, near the Chesapeake and Ohio canal, which is a small place containing but few houses, which are in a delapidated condition; also passed through JEFFERSONVILLE, a place of considerable size, very neat and comfortable in its appearance; the "Stars and Stripes," were waving from the principal buildings, and as we passed through the town, our Band playing " National airs," we were gladly welcomed by its inhabitants ; on the outskirts of the town we halted about an hour to cook dinner and rest ; resuming our march and near sundown encamped on the CARROLLTON manor, the property of the family of Charles Carroll, who was one of the signers of the "Declaration of Independence." The ground were we encamped was wet and marshy, and the water very bad. Retired to rest after a fatiguing march of 16 miles.

Sunday 18th.—Early in the morning resumed our march, passing through BUCKEYSTOWN, and crossing the bridge over the Monocacy river, encamped about two miles from the village, early in the forenoon, having marched about 5 miles.

Our camp was named in honor of Capt. Rutherford of company F.—CAMP RUTHERFORD, it is situated on a hill about a quarter of a mile from the east bank of the Monocacy, which is a shallow and narrow stream of water, and the camp was surrounded with a piece of woods, with splendid springs of water.

Pedlers both black and white, brought into camp, pies, biscuits, cooked chickens, etc., which was a change from government rations.

On the road outside of camp was a wagon with lager bier, lemonade and cakes, also a Jew pedler with tobacco, cigars, and wares of all kinds; as long the money lasted, comfort was taken but when that was gone and credit with Ralph the sutler stopped, then bean soup, hard bread, bacon, etc., and fresh meat three time, a week, took its place.

When the men were not busied with their camp duties, they employed their time in bathing in the Monocacy, rambling round the country and through the village, where we were cordially invited by the inhabitants.

Our Dress Parades was a source of interest to the numerous spectators who came a great distance to see the regiment go through its evolutions, and appeared greatly pleased with their visit.

A very sad and deplorable accident happened to a member of company B. while suffering under derangement of the mind; he loaded a musket, and placing it under his chin, pulled the trigger with his foot, and launched his soul into eternity; he was buried with military honors by his company, about a mile from camp, and in the absence of chaplain Phillips, the funeral services were performed by the Chaplain of the Twenty-ninth Pennsylania volunteers.

Company I. having been raised in New York city and attached to our regiment, arrived in camp, from Camp Cameron, Washington, D. C. where they had been detained nearly a month, they were under the command of Capt. Peter J. Claassen.

Company K. the artillery company from Rahway, N. J., were detached from the regiment, as an independent company, under the command of Captain Bunting.

But good times cannot last always, as a soldier well knows, as he is obliged to leave the comforts of camp in a good neighborhood, and take his knapsack on his back, and march wherever his orders may direct.

Monday 26th.—Late in the afternoon struck Tents, and slung knapsacks for the first time since our maiden march, the number of our wagons having been reduced; and taking our position in the Brigade, took up the line of march, passing over rough and muddy roads, many of the teams sticking fast in the mud; the night was dark and the weather chilly, and about 10 P. M. we halted and *bivouac* for the night, in a field near URBANA, Frederick County, Md., after a laborious and tedious march of 5 miles.

Tuesday 27th.—Early in the morning, after the men had breakfasted, the march was resumed over rough roads and small streams, and late in the afternoon, passed through the village of BARNESVILLE, outside of which place we encamped in a field with grain stacked, but was not allowed to use it, sleeping on the bare ground; the water was very poor, and a long distance from camp, and no permission to visit the village. We retired to rest after a tedious and rainy march of 7 miles.

Wednesday 28th.—Early in the morning again started on the march. it raining all day, and the roads were in a bad condition, passed through woods and over small streams, plodding and stumbling along till near sundown, when we encamped for the night in the vicinity of POOLESVILLE, Montgomery county, Md.,having made a disagreeable march of 10 miles.

Thursday 29th.—Early in the morning started again on the march, passing through DAWSON-VILLE, some distance from which, we took a cross road, and late in the afternoon, encamped within two miles of DARNESTOWN, having marched 8 miles.

In honor of Captain Smith of company E., our camp was named—CAMP SMITH,
and was finely situated in a cleared field, on a road branching off from the main road leading to Darnestown; in the vicinity of camp was a large

brick house, and further off was a comfortable wooden one, there was also a fine apple and peach orchard near by, and splendid springs and wells of good water, altogether it was a desirable and healthy location for a camp.

The Department was commanded by Maj. Gen. Banks, whose troops consisted of the Brigades of Abercrombie's, Williams and Hamilton's, and an independent company of infantry, known as "Collis's Zouaves," also artillery and cavalry.

Pies, biscuits, milk, cooked chickens, etc., were brought into camp for sale, by whites and blacks.

A transfer was made from the regiment to the signal corps, of two Lieutenants and six privates: First Lieutenant Charles P. Brain of company F. and Second Lieutenant William Striker, of company D. were transferred with the requisite number of privates.

Charles J. Nordquiest was appointed by Governor Morgan as regimental doctor, Howard Pinckney being his assistant, who was the only medical man with the regiment, since Doctor Bigelow left.

John Coppinger who came from home as Adjutant of the regiment, having received an appointment to a higher position, took his leave of us, with a few and affecting words, and with tears in his eyes, mounted his horse and rode away, amidst the cheers of the regiment, till he disappeared from sight. Adjutant Coppinger was beloved and respected by the rank and file of the regiment.

Charles E. Tuthill, who came from home as Second Lieutenant of company H., was appointed Adjutant, in the place of John Coppinger, resigned.

Company L. having been raised in New York city, and attached to our regiment, arrived in camp, from Camp Cameron, Washington, D. C., where they had been detained for some time, they were under the command of Captain Miller, who came from home with the regiment as First Lieutenant of company C., but had resigned; the company brought with them, the style of Tents known as the "A. Tents," and also Enfield muskets; making a full regiment of ten companies.

Company I were detailed at Maj. Gen. Banks' Head-Quarters, near Darnestown, where they remained for some time.

When off duty the time would be pleasantly spent in playing ball, and other sports of a like character; in the evening we would get an old wagon without any body, and by means of a long rope, drag it through the camp, while some one would strike on an old tin pan, to denote the district that the fire was in, and the "old truck' would go lumbering through the company's streets, upsetting the officers Tents, some of whom would enjoy the sport, while others would let their "angry passions rise," which would create shouts of laughter throughout the camp. Our sports were never prolonged to interfere with *Taps*, when every one is supposed to be in his Quarters for the night.

One evening after Dress Parade, which was visited by a number of ladies and gentlemen from Darnestown, who were invited by the field officers, to spend the evening in camp, and it being a splendid evening, the men gathered around the Colonels Quarters, and forming a ring at a respectable distance from it, commenced singing comic, national and sentimental songs ; the visitors were accommodated with camp stools, and our men gave them a musical entertainment interspersed with recitations from Shakspeare and others ; lanterns were hung from some of the tents, old bacon barrels were burnt, which threw a glare around, and all felt joyous and happy; the visitors appeared pleased and amused with the entertainment, and to give it zest, a large figure habited in the garb of a monk, made its appearance and walking around, disappeared from " whence it came," this character represented a " Knight of Malta," and was received with roars of laughter ; at an early hour the entertainment closed by the Band playing the " Star Spangled Banner," and the men retired to their Quarters. Among the visitors were noticed Brigadier General Hamilton and staff.

We gave several entertainments of a like character to the one previously spoken of, which created a reciprocal feeling between the citizens of Darnestown, and the members of the regiment, who were invited to their houses to dine with them.

Thursday September 26th.—President Lincoln having appointed this as a day of "Prayer and Fasting, for the success of our cause," about 8 A. M. formed regimental line on the parade ground, and marching through Darnestown, took our position in the Brigade, on the field were we had formerly encamped, (Camp Stone,) where the Division was formed, and the President's Proclamation was read, and prayers offered up by the Chaplains present, to the "Ruler of the Universe," who gives our armies its success or defeat; and early in the afternoon returned to camp through a heavy rain storm.

Major General Banks reviewed his Division on the field previously mentioned, a large number of spectators being present.

Received a visit from Major Sherman, who came with two months pay in "greenbacks."

One afternoon while getting ready for Battalion drill, a regiment entered camp, and halted in line facing us, and gave three years for the "New York Ninth," we returned the compliment by giving three cheers for the "Massachusetts Thirteenth," which regiment came with cordial feelings to bid us farewell, before they left for Williamsport; they marched back to their camp feeling that they were associated with their brother's of the Empire city in the same cause.

While in "Camp Smith," the anniversary day of company D. came around, the evening of which, was spent in festivities, the company's muskets were stacked in their street, and a lantern suspended from each stack, and also lanterns from Captain Greene's Tent, from which the "Lager" flowed freely, and cigars were smoked plenteously, the evening was given up to singing, and making short speeches, and the members passed a pleasant evening, nothing happening to mar their enjoyments, they retired to rest at an early hour.

There were a great deal of blustery and rainy weather, the Tents in a leaky condition, and during a rain storm very unpleasant, having to huddle together near the centre, and afraid to stir, for fear of plunging into a pool of water, and to increase your troubles, to have your Tent blow down over your heads, compelling you either to turn out and put it up, thereby getting drenched to the skin, or lay under it till morning.

Besides the usual camp duties, men were detailed for safe guards in the village of Darnestown, and also picket duty at Seneca Falls, five miles from camp.

A member of company B. having received the privilege, opened a *mess* for the officers, and also kept eatables to sell to the men.

Colonel Stiles having received a leave of absence, the command of the regiment devolved upon Lieutenant Colonel Halleck.

Monday, October 21st.—While on Battalion drill in the afternoon, orders came, to be ready to march at a moments notice, the drill was dismissed, and the men prepared for the march, and about 8 P. M., the regimental line was formed, under the command of Lieutenant Colonel Halleck, and before leaving, we burnt up all the old boxes and barrels, which illuminated the heavens around ; we were in buoyant spirits, expecting to cross into Virginia, again, and marched out of camp to join the division, our Band playing, "Carry me back to old Virginny ;" the first part of the evening was clear and the weather mild, the roads in a bad condition, and the march brisk ; passed through DAWSONVILLE, some distance from which, we came to a small, deep creek, running across the road, which either had to be forded, or crossed on a single log, reaching from one bank to the other, some distance above the water ; some took off their shoes and stockings, and waded through it, while others crossed on the log, a few falling in, the only harm they received was a good wetting; as we pursued our march passing through POOLESVILLE, we saw a guard stationed before a house, on inquiry we learned that it contained the body of Colonel Baker of the First California volunteers, who was killed that day, in the battle of BALL'S BLUFF, which was fought by Brigadier General Stone's Division, the command devolving upon Colonel Baker; now we understood why our march was hurried, it was to re-inforce Stone's Division in case of an attack the next day; we willingly quickened our speed, all along the road, men in a state of almost nudity, some with nothing more than a blanket thrown over their shoulders, still others barefooted, suffering from the cold, having swam the Potomac, near Conrad's Ferry, to prevent their being taken prisoners by the rebels, and they were going as fast as possible to Poolesville, some of them being badly wounded ; we also met government wagons filled with wounded men, going to Poolesville. Halted along the road to rest awhile, after which we crossed the Chesapeake and Ohio canal, on a boat laid across the canal, a plank reaching from the boat to the towpath, and halting long enough to load our muskets, we pursued our march quietly, the rain coming down in torrents, and about 4 A. M. halted on the banks of the Potomac, half a mile below Conrad's Ferry, and laid down in our blankets to sleep, being fatigued, after a quick march of 16 miles.

Tuesday 22.—About 9 A. M. began to stir from our wet beds, cold and hungry; hungry because we carried no rations with us, and the wagons had not yet come up, but some of the men going down the canal, came across boxes of hard bread, which they opened with their bayonets, and a party that was on picket made coffee for them, but a great many of the men, had nothing to eat. An amussing incident occurred in a house a short distance from the canal, while some of our men were eating breakfast with the family, in steps a surgeon, and told the man of the house, that he wanted "that table right away to lay a man on, whose limbs he was agoing to amputate"; the owner of the house immediately left, and it was used as a hospital.

Half a mile from where the regiment laid, was Conrad's Ferry, on the Potomac river, which is about a mile wide at that place, with Harrisons Island, in the centre, which is a small uninhabited spot of ground, and where our wounded were taken after the battle, from the Virginia shore.

The scow which had taken Colonel Baker's men across into Virginia, on the morning of the battle, was and old, decayed " dug out " which would carry about thirty men, and it was also used after the battle, in bringing the men to, and from Harrison's Island.

We planted our batteries on the eminences around Conrad's Ferry, so as to command the Virginia shore, and to protect the scow bringing the wounded men off Harrison's Island, and our Division laid along the bank of the river, which was skirted with large trees, keeping us out of sight of the rebels on the Virginia shore; we remained in that position till about noon, when the Division took up its line of march, keeping along the towpath, crossed the canal in the same place and in the same way, as the evening before, taking a road out of sight of the river, we *bivouac* towards night, in a field with grain stacked, in the vicinity of POOLESVILLE, after marching through the rain and mud, 7 miles.

After partaking of a supper of coffee and boiled salt port, laid down to sleep, some, on a straw stack, others, in a barn, while still others, slept in the open air, covered by their blankets.

Wednesday 26th.—About 3 A. M.—before daylight, was called up, and partaking of a breakfast of coffee and boiled salt pork, resumed our march, through woods and over rough roads, muddy and disagreeable, and unless you were very careful, over you would go, knapsack and all, in the mud which would cause many an execration; about 8 A. M. halted within a quarter of a mile of the Potomac, near Edward's Ferry, in a cleared field, having made a disagreeable march of 5 miles.

Towards noon, the men who fell out, having nearly all came up, we laid out camp, and pitched our Tents in a cleared field, the property of a man in the rebel service, we confiscated his wheat in the straw, to sleep on, and his rails to burn, and whatever else we could get outside of the safeguard, which was placed over his house, where his family, and overseer lived.

Near the camp was a high hill overlooking the Virginia shore, were we could see Stone's men a skirmishing with the rebels, it was really a splendid scene to witness at a distance, our men steadily advancing, their bayonets glistening in the sun, and the smoke issuing from their muskets, after firing.

Thursday 24th.—Towards evening the *long roll* was beat, and promptly falling into line, remained in that position for some time, when Colonel Stiles, who had returned from a leave of absence, addressed the regiment, saying, "that he was sorry, that he was not with the regiment at Conrad's Ferry, but as he expected the regiment to cross the river into Virginia, he hoped that every man would do his duty," the Colonel was loudly cheered, and the men were dismissed to their quarters, and ordered to sleep on their *arms*, ready to fall into line, at a moments notice ; but our slumbers were undisturbed, waking up in the morning, to find that the Union troops had recrossed the river, during the night.

Our camp was named in honor of Captain Tuthill of company H.—CAMP TUTHILL, and was finely situated, wood and water was very convenient to camp, which was situated about a quarter of a mile from the Potomac river.

Lieutenant Joseph Wickham of company H., who was home on recruiting service, arrived in, camp with a number of recruits, and he also brought with him a stand of colors, presented to the regiment by the "Common Council" of New York city.

The men that had been left in charge of Camp Cameron, Washington, D. C., when the regiment left it, re-joined the regiment, that camp having been broken up

Saturday 26th.—Early in the morning broke camp, and our Division (Banks'.) marched through

POOLESVILLE, and late in the afternoon, encamped on a hill near SENECA CREEK, after a comfortable and easy march of 10 miles.

Sunday 27th.—In the morning resumed our march, passed through DAWSONVILLE, and near DARNESTOWN, took a branch road, leading towards MUDDY BRANCH, (rightly named) near which, we halted early in the afternoon, in a piece of woods, with pine trees and brushes, and clearing them away, we laid out camp, in low, marshy ground. Marched that day, 10 miles.

In honor of Captain Prescott of company C., our camp was named—CAMP PRESCOTT, it was in an unhealthy, muddy, and watery place; and the water for cooking and drinking purposes, was very impure.

The stand of colors given to the regiment by the "Common Council" of the city of New York, was presented on Dress Parade by Lieutenant Wickham, in their behalf, to Colonel Stiles in behalf of the regiment, with an appropriate speech, which was replied to by the Colonel, and three cheers were given for the donors.

Company I. who were detailed at Major General Banks' Head Quarters, re-joined the regiment. which they had left at Camp Smith.

We had a great deal of rainy and damp weather, and our Tents leaked badly, there was a great deal of sickness throughout the regiment, and Doctor Nordquiest representing that fact, to the General, advised the removal of camp, to higher and healthier grounds, so therefore on the afternoon of

Tuesday, November 5th., moved out of the woods, to a cleared field, a short distance from Camp Prescott, there the regiment was more healthy, the camp being on higher ground.

Wednesday 20th.—Early in the morning, the Brigade crossed to the other side of MUDDY BRANCH, and encamped on the direct road to Darnestown, distant about two miles, having marched 4 miles.

A sad accident happened to private Ferrero of company A., one day, while setting in his Tent; through the carelessness of some person in discharging his musket, a ball passed through Ferrero's Tent, wounding him in the leg, he was carried on a stretcher to the camp hospital, and sometime afterwards received his discharge from the United States service.

Sunday 24th.—The first fall of snow the season, the weather cold and wet.

Details were made from the regiment to work on fortifications, and also to do picket duty along the canal.

Thursday 28th.—Thanksgiving day at home,

all drills dispensed with, and the men permitted to leave the camp to spend the day, while those who could not afford it, had their Thanksgiving dinner in camp, of Government rations—Bean soup and hard bread.

Monday, December 2d.—After breakfast struck Tents, and leaving a detail behind to take care of the sick, and to guard part of the camp left behind, as the roads were in a bad condition; took up our position in the Division, the pioneer corps, composed of men detailed from each regiment in the Brigade, going in advance, constructing temporary bridges of rails, for the Division to cross over, and making roads; the weather was cold and freezing, the march tedious, and towards evening we pitched our Tents near BARNESVILLE for the night, making a march of 17 miles.

Tuesday 3d.—Early in the morning resumed the march, under the same difficulties as the day previous; passed in sight of Sugar Loaf mountain where our signal corps was stationed, and pursuing our march passed Camp Rutherford, near the Monocacy river, passing through BUCKEYS-TOWN, and late in the afternoon pitched our Tents, in a piece of woods, near Frederick Junction, making a march of 16 miles.

Wednesday 4th.—Late in the forenoon, broke camp, and resumed our march, taking the road leading to IAMESVILLE, encamped early in the afternoon, in a piece of woods within two miles of that place, and five miles west of FREDERICK city, making a march of 7 miles.

From Aug. 17th to Dec. 4th 1861, the regiment made fifteen marches travelling 143 miles.

CHAPTER III.

From December 4, 1861, *to February* 25, 1862.

In honor of Captain Claassen of company I., the camp was named—CAMP CLAASSEN, it was situated on the road leading to IAMESVILLE, distant two miles, and was a healthy situation, the water was good and convenient to camp, in the vicinity of which, were several dwelling houses.

The day after we encamped, everything that we left behind at Muddy Branch, arrived in camp, the sick was brought to the Point-of-Rocks, on a canal boat, under the medical charge of Assistant Surgeon Pinckney, and from there, they were taken to the United States Army Hospital at Frederick city, where Doctor Pinckney, was detailed.

The men cleared the wood from the encampment, using the logs to build their winter quarters with, filling up the cracks between the logs, with mud, making the floors with boards purchased in Frederick city, and buying small sheet iron stoves, to warm our houses with, so that we made ourselves quite comfortable for the winter.

There were three passes granted to each company, daily, to visit Frederick city, till sundown, and an enterprising citizen, started a stage from our camp to the city, which was patronized by the members of the regiment.

FREDERICK city, situated in Frederick county, Md., on the Monocacy river, about four miles from Frederick Junction, which is on the Baltimore and Ohio railroad, a branch of which, runs to the city; it contains some very fine buildings, and had the appearance of having been a thriving place, previous to the Rebellion. The inhabitants are hospitable, and the majority are loyal, visiting our hospital, bringing delicacies to the poor sick soldiers; the ladies of Frederick city, will be remembered by the soldiers, long after the Rebellion has ceased.

Major General Banks, made his Head-Quarters in Frederick city, at the residence of Bradley Johnson, a Colonel in the rebel service.

Pedlers frequented camp with eatables, besides which, there was the "Ark" man, who gave the men credit, till pay-day, a loyal refugee from Virginia, who opened an oyster saloon, in a Tent, near the camp, a man from the city taking ambrotypes and views of the camp, and to conclude with, there was Ralph, our enterprising sutler, all of whom, lightened our pockets considerably.

A commissioned officer with a number of men, were detailed to examine passes of soldiers on the cars, as they stopped at Frederick Junction.

The camp hospital was situated, within a quarter of a mile from camp, in a two story frame house, part of which was occupied by a colored family, who gave up the front room on the first floor, and also the second story, for our sick, which were but few, as the regiment was pretty healthy.

Sergeant Frank G. Aims, of company D., died in the hospital at Frederick city, an escort from his company, left camp for Frederick Junction, where the body of their late comrade-in-arms, arrived in a wagon from Frederick city, the coffin was opened, and taking a last look of their dear comrade, the coffin was closed, and the body in charge of First Sergeant Lanning, proceeded to New York city. Sergeant Aims, was loved and respected by all of his company, who drew up resolutions of sympathy and condolence, which were printed in Frederick city, by three members of his company, and copies forwarded to his friends and relatives.

The Division was reviewed by Major General Banks, our regiment marching through the city, the Band playing its liveliest tunes, and the people thronged the streets to see us, as we passed through, and marching to a field on the outskirts of the city, we were reviewed, and returned to camp, being tired and hungry.

We stationed a picket at Monocacy Ford, about two miles from camp, to search all wagons coming in the direction of camp, for liquors, and to examine the passes of all soldiers, going towards Frederick city.

Wednesday, December 25th.—Christmas-day rolls around, and calls to remembrance a year ago, when our country was at peace, and the soldiers were at their homes, enjoying themselves around the firesides, with their friends and companions, but the times are changed, the land is at strife with its rebellious brother, and the scenes of the firesides, is changed to the camp with its rough associations; the usual drills being dispensed with for the day, the men gave themselves up to innocent sports, such as horse, foot and sack racings, Major Atterbury taking the lead in these amusements, and some of the companies had good christmas dinner's furnished from their company's fund, and it was cooked outside of camp; while others, had a christmas-dinner of bean soup and hard bread; although the camp was muddy and disagreeable, still the day passed off pleasantly. In the morning, at the camp hospital, private Leonard Rodgers of company D., died, after a short illness, his sister who came to see him, was about returning home, when her brother died, and

Thursday 26th.—In the afternoon, company D. paraded, to pay due respects to their late comrade in-arms, private Leonard Rogers, who died the day previous, the funeral service was performed by Chaplain Phillips on the parade ground, the ensign lowered at half-mast, and after the service, an escort from the company, followed the ambulance, containing the body of the deceased, and his sister, to Frederick Junction, to take the cars for New York city. The escort remained with the body till the next morning, when his sister, and private McNally of company D., left for home with the body.

Several days after, an escort was sent from company H. to the Junction, to pay respects to the remains of their late comrade-in arms, private William Miller, who died in the hospital at Frederick city, and whose body was sent home in charge of private William O'Brien.

Sergeant Dennin of company H., was sent to Alexandria, Va., where he took charge of the body of private John Caffery, who died in the Army Hospital at that place, conveying the remains home to his friends.

Wednesday, January 1st. 1862.—New-Years day, the same as any other to the inhabitants of Maryland, whose festive day is Christmas, but we could not forget the *New Year's calls* of the year before, and the enjoyments with friends, but passed the day away pleasantly in innocent amusements, similar to those of Christmas-day.

Friday 3d.—Vice President Hamlin, and Major General Rosecrans visited, Frederick city, to whom an entertainment was given, and the officers of our regiment, and also our Band, were invited to attend, which invitation they accepted.

Monday 6th.—In the afternoon received a visit from ex-adjutant Coppinger, and before Dress Parade was dismissed, Sergeant Strong of company F. in a short speech, presented in behalf of the non-commissioned officers and privates of the regiment, a splendid sword and sash, with its appendages, to ex-adjutant Coppinger, as a testimonial of his worth and esteem; the recipient replied in a few feeling remarks. This gift was gotten up at Camp Smith, by the non-commissioned officers and privates, of the regiment, by subscription, and cost $250, with a splendid inscription engraved thereon.

Before leaving camp, ex-adjutant Coppinger, passed through all of the companies' streets, from which he was loudly cheered; the men gathered around the Colonel's quarters, and the cry resounded, Coppinger! Coppinger! a speech! a speech! making his appearance, he made a few remarks, after which a cry was raised for a speech from Colonel Stiles, the Colonel appeared, and saying a few words, bade ex-adjutant Coppinger farewell, who entered his carriage, and rode away, while the regiment cheered boisterously till he was out of sight.

Tuesday 7th.—A day of sad and distressing news, throwing a dark shadow over the regiment.—News was received in camp, that our beloved Lieutent Colonel, William Halleck, who was home on a leave of absence, died of consumption, while surrounded by his family; often in Camp Smith, when every thing was quiet, could be heard his coughing, whilst others slept, and the night that we left that camp, expecting to cross into Virginia, he commanded the regiment in the absence of the Colonel, and the next day when companies A. D. and L., were ordered to cross over to Harrison's Island, he was eager to command them, but Brigadier General Stone, knowing that it would be certain destruction to do so, countermanded the order. Lieutenant Colonel Halleck wished to lay his life down for his country, and was willing to die on the field of battle. The officers met and passed resolutions of sympathy and condolence, which were sent to the bereaved family of their respected Lieutenant Colonel.

First Sergeant Lanning, after his election as

First Lieutenant of company D., was presented by Sergeant Claire, in behalf of the non-commissioned officers and privates of the company, with a splendid sword and sash, purchased in Frederick city, the recipient replied to the speech in a few, but appropriate words.

Near the middle of the month, Major Sherman, again, made his appearance with the "greenbacks," to pay us the two months pay due us.

Doctor Nordquiest having been taken sick, received a leave of absence to visit his home, to recruit his health, his place was taken by Assistant Surgeon Pinckney, who had been detailed in the hospital at Frederick city, and after Doctor Nordquiest returned, he resumed his duties.

The weather was very changeable, some days it would be nice and dry, at others, cold and wet, there were several snow storms, and our regiment was pretty healthy.

We encamped in a thick woods, but it did not last long, as we had to send our teams a long distance from camp, to get wood to burn and do our cooking with.

When the weather permitted, the usual drills were gone through with, some of the streets were corduroyed with logs, making them less muddy, than they otherwise would be.

When their duties were done, the men would

amuse themselves by playing ball, pitching quoits, and other sports of a like character, which would pass away the *ennui* of camp life.

Orders were received from the War Department, for sea-faring men, to volunteer to man the gun-boats, on the Western rivers, to rendezvous at Cairo, Illinois; privates Gray of company C, Jaques of D., Sands of E., Pinard of H., Boker of I. and Watson of L , volunteered, and were accepted, making the requisite number required from our regiment; they were forwarded to Frederick city, and with others from the Division, was sent west.

On being mustered into the United States service, we were guaranteed our Militia rights, of electing our own officers, which right, was violated by Governor Morgan, in appointing Major Atterbury as Lieutenant Colonel, to fill the vacancy caused by the death of Lieutenant Colonel Halleck, and also appointing Captain Rutherford of company F., as Major of the " Eighty-third New York volunteers, being the first official intimation, that we had, of the " Ninth New York State Militia," being submerged into that organization, which never existed. This order created a great deal of dissatisfaction amongst the men and officers, who were determined to preserve the " Ninth" intact, and if possible to win a name for it, in the annals of our country's history, of the Southern Rebellion.

Saturday, February 22d.—Washington's birthday—was kept as a holiday, all drills dispensed with, and the day passed away pleasantly in playing ball, and sports of a like character.

Number of times we received orders to cook rations and be ready for marching, but the orders were all countermanded, and we remained quietly in our comfortable quarters.

In winter quarters from December 4th., 1861, to February 25th,, 1862, when the spring campaign commenced under Major General Banks.

CHAPTER IV.

From *February* 25, *to May* 29., 1862.

Tuesday, February 25th.—Early in the morning broke camp, and marched a mile and a half to IAMESVILLE, and taking the cars from there to SANDY HOOK, distant 23 miles, arrived early in the afternoon, and encamped on Maryland Heights, on our old camp ground, (Camp Davis,) where we remained for the night.

Wednesday 26th.—In the afternoon, the Division marched to the Potomac river, and crossed the *Pontoon* bridge at HARPER'S FERRY, where the river is little over a mile wide, found the place deserted, and the United States Government factory of muskets and fire-arms, entirely destroyed, and the machinery carried away; marched on till we came to BOLIVAR, where we quartered for the night, in the deserted houses, after having marched 5 miles.

On our approach to Bolivar, the inhabitants of Secession proclivities, made a hurried flight, leaving their hogs and chickens, behind them, which we confiscated for our own use.

Friday 28th.—Shortly after sundown, left our quarters, and the Division marched without halting, till they reached CHARLESTOWN, where we stood in the streets over an hour, the night piercing cold, and the men suffered severely from it; countermarched and *bivouac* in the woods, about half a mile from the town, having marched in one hour and fifty minutes, 8 miles.

Saturday, March 1st.—Laid out camp, and companies D. and E., with a squadron from the First Michigan cavalry, were detailed to go to Leetown, distant 6 miles, on picket duty.

While laying near Charlestown, had a heavy fall of snow, the weather cold and disagreeable.

Our Wall Tents were taken from us, in place of which, we received the Sibley's, which would hold twenty men, on a squeeze.

The officers *mess* was broken up, after leaving our winter quarters at Camp Claassen.

Thursday 6th.—Early in the morning, bid adieu to Charlestown, where we had been encamped, nearly a week, and taking up our position in the Division, took up the line of march, passing through a fine and fertile country, and over good roads, and towards evening, encamped near MIDDLEWAY; the day was clear, and we made an easy march of 8 miles.

While we remained encamped near Middleway, two men belonging to the Twenty-seventh Indiana volunteers, (of our Brigade,) while foraging the country, were attacked by rebel cavalry, one was shot, and the other taken prisoner, the Union cavalry pursued and overtook the rebel cavalry, and captured two of them.

Monday 10th.—Early in the morning, broke camp, and taking our position in the Division, marched over rough and muddy roads, and late in the afternoon, encamped near the village of BUNKER HILL, after a tedious and disagreeable march of 6 miles.

That night after we had encamped, companies D. and E. returned from picket duty at Leetown, where they went from the camp near Charlestown, they found Leetown, to be a small village containing but few houses, the inhabitants hospitable and friendly ; they took up their quarters in a house and barn ; and on the morning of the 10th., started to return to the regiment, which they joined that evening, in camp near Bunker Hill.

One of the men of the Twenty-ninth Pennsylvania volunteers, (of our Brigade,) while on picket near our camp, was shot by a hidden foe, not being conscious of any, in the vicinity of camp.

Tuesday 11th.—About noon broke camp, and taking our position in the Division, marched through the village of BUNKER HILL, and crossed a bridge, hastily thrown over a small stream, by the pioneers ; marched on the Winchester pike, which is a splendid level road, and passing through a fine, fertile, and well watered country, surrounded by splendid sceneries; on the march our cavalry, made a sudden dash upon a small body of rebel cavalry, within a few miles of Winchester, and drove them through the town, but night approaching, our cavalry left off pursuing them, and fell back outside of the town; at nightfall the Division *bivouac* within five miles of Winchester, and slept on their *arms*, ready in case of an attack, to repel it at once. Our march was a fatiguing one, of 12 miles.

Wednesday 12th.—In the morning, the Division resumed its march, moving slowly and cautiously along, expecting an attack every moment, but on reaching Winchester, we found that under cover of the night, General Jackson's rebel forces, had evacuated the place, many of the male inhabitants leaving with him, while he carried away with him, a few Union men, to prevent them from giving information; we found that the place had been strongly fortified, and passing through it, halted on the outskirts, early in the day, and pitched our Tents, on the Strasburg pike, on an elevated piece of land, overlooking Winchester, where we sent out our pickets, and detailed company H., to do provost duty, in the town. Our march was about 6 miles that day.

WINCHESTER, is the county town of Frederick county, Va., in the Shenandoah valley, the Winchester and Potomac railroad running through the town, it contained previous to the rebellion, about eight thousand inhabitants, the male portion of which, are mostly in the rebel service; it had the appearance of having been a thriving place.

One day while laying encamped near Winchester, the *long roll* was beat, the regiment fell in to line, and double-quicked it about two miles, when it was ascertained, that our cavalry pickets, had been driven in, by a body of rebel cavalry, our cavalry being reinforced, drove them back, capturing a number of them, and all becoming quiet along the lines, we returned to camp.

The regiment received another friendly visit from the " Thirteenth Massachusetts," which was a repetition of the one, they made us at Camp Smith, near Darnestown, Maryland.

Number of visitors from Winchester and its vicinity, visited camp to see the regiment go through its evolutions on Dress Parade, and compare our neat and comfortable appearance, with the dirty and slovenly appearance of the rebels.

The weather was very changeable, cold one day, and warm the next, then, a spell of rainy weather, then, came a short season of dry weather, and take it in all, it was very disagreeable and unhealthy weather.

Friday 21st.—In the morning our regiment, joined Brigadier General Abercrombie's Brigade, composed of the Twelfth and Thirteenth Massachusetts and the Twelfth and Sixteenth Indiana volunteers, which Brigade was detached from Major General Banks' Division, forming an independent command, known as the "light Brigade," which took up its line of march, and halted near a small stream, while the pioneers cut down trees to make a bridge, so that we might cross over; pursued our march, crossing the bridge, and passing through a fertile, and well watered country, and towards evening, *bivouac* near BERRYVILLE, 11 miles to the eastward of Winchester, after a march over muddy roads, and through the rain.

Saturday 22d.—In the morning resumed the march, cossing the Shenandoah river, on a *Pontoon* bridge, hastily constructed by the "Sixteenth Indiana," and towards evening, pitched our Tents, on the BLUE RIDGE Mountain, near SNICKERSVILLE, which is in the western part of Loudon county, Va. Our march was over good roads, the weather cold but clear, and marching 7 miles.

Sunday 23d.—Early in the morning, resumed

our march, taking the Aldee pike, and crossing Goose Creek bridge, passed through the village of ALDEE, on the outskirts of which, late in the afternoon, we encamped, having marched 17 miles.

Monday 24th.—Late in the afternoon, the Brigade marched towards Winchester, to reinforce the troops of Brigadier General Shields, the night was extremely cold, and starlight; and marching till day-break, the next morning, *bivouac* along the road, to get a little sleep and rest, having made a fatiguing march of 18 miles.

Tuesday 25th.—Early in the afternoon resumed our march towards Winchester, which had been delayed by the breaking down of the bridge, crossing the Shenandoah river; marched about two miles, when the news was brought, that Shields' men, had repulsed General Jackson's rebel forces, gaining a complete victory over him, which news was received by us, with great rejoicings, and countermarching, we encamped for the night, on the BLUE RIDGE Mountain, having marched 5 miles.

Wednesday 26th.—Marched early in the morning, and crossing the Blue Ridge Mountain, late in the afternoon, encamped in the woods, on the Aldee pike, near GOOSE CREEK bridge, after a weary and fatiguing march of 12 miles.

We had been encamped but a short time, when the *long roll* was beat, and Colliss's Zouaves, of General Banks' body guards, and the Twelfth Massachusetts volunteers, of our Brigade, started in pursuit of some rebel cavalry, that had been hovering around; marching about 7 miles, towards Middlebury, and meeting nothing, they returned to their camps.

We would not give our readers to understand, because we are called the "light Brigade," that we travel in "light marching orders," but far from it, beside our muskets and forty rounds of cartridges, there is a heavy knapsack on your back, and three days rations in your haversack.

Friday 28th.—In the forenoon, our Brigade took up its line of march, along the Aldee pike, passing through a fertile, and well watered country, and after a laborious march, we encamped late in the afternoon, on the plains of MANASSAS, within 4 miles of Centreville, near a splendid stream of water; this is a level plain as far as the eye can see, dotted here and there, with farm houses. Marched that day 14 miles.

Saturday 29th.—Early in the morning, resumed our march, passing through CENTREVILLE, where we saw the abandoned earth-works and rifle-pits, of the rebels; pursuing our march, we crossed Bull Run Creek, on a bridge, re-built where the old one stood, which was burnt by the rebels on their retreat; after crossing the bridge, marched about two miles, and night coming on, we pitched our Tents, in a low, swampy place, near MANASSAS, having marched through the hail and snow, 8 miles.

Sunday 30th.—The weather rainy, still it did not hinder us from pursuing our march at an early hour; the roads were in a bad condition; and early in the day, we encamped near MANASSAS JUNCTION, where we saw the abandoned earth works and rifle-pits of the rebels, who had been strongly fortified, before they evacuated it. Our march was a light one, of 4 miles.

Monday 31st.—There being no "rest for the weary," and no signs of any, for the poor, worn out soldier, we obeyed the commands to march early in the morning, passing through a barren, and poorly watered country, and crossing Broad Run, on a single log, late in the afternoon, pitched our Tents, near that stream, after marching 12 miles.

Tuesday, April 1st.—Early in the morning, the Brigade resumed its march, along the Orange and Alexandria railroad, passed through CATTLET'S station, crossed the stream on logs laid across, by our pioneers, as the rebels had destroyed the railroad bridge, on their retreat; the aspect of the country, began to change, to a fertile and well watered country, with splendid sceneries; leaving the railroad, and taking a cross road leading to WEAVERSVILLE, near which place, we pitched our Tents, towards night, on a cleared field. The weather was clear and fine, and the march was an easy one, of 10 miles.

Wednesday 2d.—Early in the day, pursued our march, and encamped in the woods, near WARRENTON JUNCTION, after a short march of 4 miles.

A *reconnoissance* under Colonel Lucas of the Sixteenth Indiana volunteers, with a company, from each regiment in the Brigade, (company L., of our regiment.) with a squadron of cavalry, and a section of artillery, started for Rappahannock Station, distant 10 miles, where they destroyed the abandoned earth-works of the rebels, North of the Rappahannock river, and they then returned to camp from which they had been absent, about forty-eight hours, it hailing hard most of the time.

Company H. which had been left at Winchester doing provost duty, returned to the regiment.

While laying in camp, had a heavy fall of snow and the weather was pretty cool, that time of year.

Saturday 12th.—Our camping ground being unhealthy, and badly situated on account of water, we moved camp about a mile, on cleared land, near a splendid creek, where the water was good, and in sufficient quantities.

Received a visit from Major Sherman, who gave us the two months pay due us.

For the first time since entering the United States service, the light blue pants, were drawn from the Government, and worn in the place of the dark blue pants, with red stripes, we also donned the overcoats, at Camp Claassen, Md., leaving us only our fatigue jackets, as the only apparel, denoting our original uniform.

Brigadier General Abercrombie, having been relieved by Brigadier General Hartsuff, reviewed the Brigade, before taking his leave.

Another *reconnoissance* was made to Rappahannock Station, under the command of Lieutenant Colonel Brien of the Twelfth Massachusetts volunteers, with five companies from each regiment of the Brigade, also cavalry and artillery; they left camp one morning, about nine o'clock, and made a steady march, till they reached the Station, when the artillery was planted on an eminence, and fired a few shells into the rebel camps, on the South side of the Rappahannock river, as they were mounting guards for the day, which took them by surprise, scattering them promiscuously; after which, our men marched back to camp, having been away forty-eight hours.

marching steady night and day, 20 miles, and on

Monday, May 5th.—Early in the morning, the Brigade, under command of Brigadier General George L. Hartsuff, marched towards CAT-LETT'S Station, where shortly after noon, we encamped on an eminence, commanding a splendid view of the surrounding country ; making a short march of 4 miles.

In honor of the then, Secretary of War, the Hon. Edwin M. Stanton, our camp was named

CAMP STANTON,

it was splendidly situated, and nicely laid out, a fine spring of water, near by, and a nice, clear creek to bathe in ; the trees were in full bloom, and the grass was clothed in its green verdure, making the surrounding sceneries, enchanting to the sight.

While remaining encamped, our Brigade was reviewed by Brigadier General Hartsuff.

Monday 12th.—About noon the Brigade took up its line of march, the weather warm, and the roads dusty, the men suffered from the intense heat, and for the want of water; and towards evening, pitched our tents on cleared ground, near a small creek, having made a disagreeable and fatiguing march of 8 miles.

Tuesday 13th.—Resuming our march early in the morning, passed through a fine country, but poorly watered, the weather was warm and sultry, and the roads dusty, and towards night, we encamped near HARTWOOD Church, located in Stafford county, after a tedious march of 15 miles.

Wednesday 14th.--On the road again, at an early hour, the weather rainy, and the roads muddy, passed through the small village of HARTWOOD, and towards evening passed through FALMOUTH, and encamped about a mile from the Rappahannock river, nearly opposite Fredericksburg. Laid down to rest, being drenched to the skin, and worn out, after a disagreeable march of 10 miles.

FALMOUTH, situated in the South-western part of Stafford county, Va., on the North side of the Rappahannock river, was a place of considerable importance, the Acquia Creek and Potomac railroad, passing through the town. There was a large iron railroad bridge, besides two other bridges, all crossing the Rappahannock river, which were destroyed by the rebels, on their retreat to the South side of the river.

The Eleventh Pennsylvania volunteers, took the place in the Brigade, of the Twelfth and Sixteenth Indiana volunteers, whose time having expired, went home while at Catlett's Station.

Since encamping near Falmouth, we came under the Department, denominated as the " Army of the Potomac," under the command of Major General McDowell; the Division, under Brigadier General Ord; and the Brigade composed of the Twelfth and Thirteenth Massachusetts, and the Eleventh Pennsylvania volunteers, and our regiment, under the command of Brigadier General Hartsuff; which troops were reviewed by Major General McDowell.

Saturday 17th—On account of water being poor and scarce, and also an unhealthy camping ground, we moved about a mile further down the river, and encamped on a cleared field, where was a good spring near by, and also a sulphur spring.

There were issued to each man, one half of a SHELTER TENT, which are pieces of canvass, two being joined together, making a Tent large enough for two men to crawl in, and sleep under, to take the place of the Sibley Tents.

One day, double-quicked it about a mile, when we found President Lincoln, and the Secretary of of War, Hon. Edwin M Stanton, waiting to review Major General McDowell's troops.

Major Sherman paid us a welcome visit, dispensing the " green-backs" for our pay.

Orders were issued to our Brigade, that we should march six miles every day while laying in camp, with packed knapsacks, to accustom ourselves to the hardships of marching ; pursuant to such orders, we marched to Bell's landing, and back again, making 12 miles. Also had knapsack drill every morning.

Sunday 25th.—In the afternoon, our Brigade marched towards Acquia creek, over rough roads, through woods, up hills and down dales, and nearing ACQUIA creek, about midnight, laid down near the road, fatigued with a quick march of 15 miles.

Monday 26th.—A great number of the men having fallen out from fatigued, reached their commands, when the Brigade marched down to the creek, and embarked on the steamboat South America, which transferred us to the steamer Vanderbilt, laying outside, after which proceeded up the Potomac river, and ran aground near Indian Head, where we remained all night. A tow-boat came out to us with rations, as we had had nothing to eat, since leaving camp at Falmouth, the afternoon previous. The decks were wet and uncomfortable, and pretty well crowded for a night's rest.

Tuesday 27th.—A year ago, the regiment left New York city, expecting to return in a few months. but on this, their anniversary day, they find themselves on a steamer, in the Potomac

4*

river, aground, but the steamer Red Jacket, came to our relief, taking us off from the Vanderbilt, and landing us at Alexandria, Va., about noon. After landing, we marched through the city, outside of which, we encamped. Our men rambled through the city, commemorating their anniversary day, and having a good time in general. Towards evening, those that could be gathered together, took the cars for Manassas Junction, distant 27 miles, and on arriving there, slept in the cars till the next morning.

Wednesday 28th.—Leaving the cars in the morning, marched about 2 miles, and encamped near the railroad.

From Feb. 25th to May 29th, 1862, the regiment made twenty-three marches, travelling 218 miles.

CHAPTER V.

From May 29, to September 6, 1862.

Friday 30th.—In the morning, our Division took up its line of march, and passing through GAINESVILLE, took the cars to HAYMARKET, the other side of which, the bridge crossing Broad Run creek, had been destroyed by the rebels, and leaving the cars there, forded the creek, and passed through THOROUGH-FARE Gap, the roads dry, and the weather warm; towards night encamped in an orchard, having rode in the cars 5 miles, and marched about 7 miles.

Saturday 31st.—In the morning resumed our march, along the Manassas Gap railroad, it raining hard throughout the day; and passing through the small villages of WHITE PLAINS, and SALEM, and late in the afternoon, encamped in a field with standing grass, on the suburbs of the latter place. Our rubber blankets were the only articles between us and the wet grass, and we courted repose after a weary march of 10 miles.

Sunday, June 1st.—In the morning, took up the line of march, along the Manassas Gap railroad, till we came to the village of PIEDMONT, where we halted for several hours, when resuming the march, leaving a guard in the railroad depot, with our knapsacks, taking nothing but our haversacks and blankets with us, we passed through the small villages of MARKHAM, LINDEN, and several others, and fording several small streams on our route, passed through MANASSAS Gap, a pass in the Blue Ridge Mountains, and after dark *bivouac* in the woods near FRONT ROYAL. It was a rainy day, and the night was tempestuous, and the men scattered themselves, to find comfort if they could, from the drenching rain, after a laborious and muddy march of 17 miles.

Monday 2d.—Resumed our march in the morning, passing FRONT ROYAL, marched about two miles towards the Shenandoah river, and *bivouac* early in the day, on a hill, near the junction of the North and South forks of the river. To make ourselves comfortable, we confiscated the rails and boards, in the vicinity of camp, for shelter and to cook with. We made a short march of 5 miles.

Wednesday 4th —Early in the morning, took up the line of march, along the railroad, and crossed the Shenandoah river, near which stream, early in the day, we *bivouac* in a cluster of pines and cedars; the forenoon was warm and clear; and the afternoon rainy, continuing through the night. The march was a short one, of 5 miles.

Thurday 5th.—Resumed our march, early in the morning, and *bivouac* early in the day, in the woods, within a mile of the bridge crossing the South Fork of the Shenandoah River, having made a short march of 5 miles.

Friday 6th.—In the morning, marched back towards the Shenandoah river, and crossing the bridge, *bivouac* early in the afternoon, in the woods, within a mile of FRONT ROYAL, having marched 8 miles.

FRONT ROYAL, the county town of Warren county, Va., situated on the Manassas Gap railroad, and but a short distance from the Shenandoah river; was a place of considerable size and importance, previous to the rebellion, and lays in the fertile and beautiful valley of the Shenandoah.

While laying encamped, our knapsacks which was left at Piedmont, in charge of men detailed for that purpose, arrived, when we laid out camp.

Brigadier General Ord, commanding our division, was relieved by Brigadier General Ricketts who had commanded a brigade in the Division, and who was wounded and taken prisoner, at the first battle of Bull Run, while in command of a battery, known as "Ricketts Battery,,' of which he was Captain.

Tuesday 17th.—In the morning marched to

FRONT ROYAL, and took the cars from there to Manassas Junction, a distance of 52 miles; left the cars, and marched about 2 miles, and late in the afternoon encamped on an open field, within three miles of the "First Bull Run" battle ground.

Friday, July 4th.—While the men were celebrating, the day of their country's independence, their sports about noon, was interrupted by the orders "to pack up," and marching through a hot, broiling sun, passed through GAINESVILLE, and about sundown, encamped in an open field, about a mile from that place, having marched 12 miles.

Saturday 5th·—Resumed our march early in the morning, the heat very oppressive, forded a large stream running across the road, passed through NEW BALTIMORE, and late in the afternoon encamped in an open field, about a mile from WARRENTON, having marched 10 miles.

Heard of the death of Henry L. Stevens, who came from home with the regiment, as Quartermaster; he having received a leave of absence, died at home, of consumption, surrounded by his family and friends ; his loss was deeply regretted, by the regiment, which had lost an efficient officer.

Colonel Stiles appointed, First Lieutenant A. Martin Burtis of company L., as Quartermaster, he having been acting as such, during the sickness of the late Quartermaster.

WARRENTON, the county town of Fauquier county, nine miles from Warrenton Junction, which lays on the Orange and Alexandria railroad, a branch running to Warrenton, which was a splendid little city, containing about eight thousand inhabitants, most of the males were in the rebel service; there were some fine buildings, and several splendid churches, which were used as hospitals; there was a large grave yard, containing the graves of a great many rebel and Union soldiers, laying side by side, until the day of resurrection. The inhabitants were rank disunionists, rejoicing in their sentiments, and abhorring the "old flag," under which their ancestors, had lived and died.

A little distance from Warrenton, was the Palatial residence of extra-Billy Smith, well known some years ago, on the floors of Congress, his family resides here in perfect security, while he is in the confederacy, helping his brothers, of the same stripe, in their accursed conclave, to dismember the union.

Captain Bates, of the Twelfth Massachusetts volunteers, was appointed Provost Marshall of the city of Warrenton, with his company, and company C. of our regiment, which were quartered in the deserted houses, Captain Bates office was in the City Hall, a large stone building, on Main street.

Major General John C. Pope, was here, assigned to the command of the Department of the "Army of Virginia," comprising all the troops around Warrenton and its vicinity.

About the middle of July, "the Army" began its march, leaving onr regiment, and a small body of cavalry, at Warrenton; Colonel Stiles was appointed Military Commander of the Post, and Captain Hendrickson of company G., was appointed Provost Marshall; the regiment broke camp, and took up their quarters, in the deserted houses in the city, but the weather being too warm, they encamped in different places outside of the city, while the Colonel took up his quarters in a private dwelling.

The regiment's duties, were doing provost duty, loading cars, tending the hospitals, which were moving to the rear, as fast as possible.

Our Dress Parades and Guard Mountings, took place on Main street, the band playing National "Airs," at first, there could not be seen a female, in the street, but casting your eyes up towards the windows, they could be seen peeping through the blinds, but in a few evenings, they came boldly out, and could be seen talking with our men, and witnessing our evolutions.

A member of company D. while rambling through the city one day, came across the office formerly occupied by the "Warrenton Whig," on entering, he discovered a Washington hand press, and on the imposing stone, was a reprint in type of the *Richmond Dispatch*; leaving the office, and pursuing his investigations further, he found printing materials secreted in different parts of the city, and moving them to the office, associated with him, a member of company L., and they sent to Washington, After paper, and shortly afterwards, appeared a little sheet, called the "New York Ninth," and of the first number was issued two editions, one of fifteen hundred, and the other, of one thousand copies, it passed through the second number, issuing two thousand copies, when the regiment was ordered to join the Brigade.

The members of the regiment, held several musical *soirees*, in an enclosure belonging to the Warrenton Hotel, the ladies were invited to attend, the Programmes were printed in good style, and consisted of comic and sentimental songs, recitations from Shakespeare and others; the Band discoursed sweet music to the admiring ear, playing National "Airs," and lively tunes; the performances were harmoniously conducted, and the entertainments concluded with a good feeling existing between the people and the members of the "New York Ninth."

Tuesday, August 5th.--Major Rutherford took

command of the regiment, Colonel Stiles not having been relieved from his command of Military Commander, and Lieutenant Colonel Atterbury, being sick; the regiment marched early in the morning, and halted for several hours at SULPHUR SPRINGS, seven miles from Warrenton. These springs previous to the rebellion, was a great place of resort for the *elite* of Warrenton and its vicinity; there was a hotel, with other large buildings, which had been entirely destroyed. Resuming our march, crossed the North branch of the Rappahannock river, and marching about two miles further, encamped late in the afternoon, in a cluster of pines, the weather clear and warm, having marched 10 miles.

Wednesday 6th.—In the morning continued the march, through a hot, broiling sun, and towards evening encamped within a mile of CULPEPPER, where we re-joined the Brigade. This was an uncomfortable march of 15 miles.

Friday 8th.— Towards noon, the Division took up its line of march, passing through CULPEPPER, and halted for several hours in a thick pine woods, the sun hot, and not a breath of wind stirring, and towards evening, marched a little further, when we encamped, in an open field, having marched 5 miles.

Saturday 9th.—At day-break, broke camp, and

marched about two miles, when we halted in a narrow dirt road, unprotected from the hot, broiling sun; there we drew rations, being hungry for the want of them; heavy cannonading was heard near by, when the news was brought, that Bank's troops, were engaged with the rebels at CEDAR Mountain, about 5 miles distant; late in the afternoon, Major Generals Pope and McDowell, rode by, and our Division comprising the Brigades of Tower's, Duryea's and Hartsuff's, fell in to line, and made a quick march of two miles. when they halted in a field near the road, and stacking their *arms*, unslung knapsacks, and detailed a guard to remain in charge of them, and taking up their *arms*, filed into the road, making a quick march towards where the contest was raging; the roar of artillery was heard nearer, and nearer, as we advanced; halted, and stacked arms for a few moments, when making a quick march, we neared the field of action, the night being moonlight, our bayonets glistened in the light, that, and one of the Bands in Carroll's Brigade, commencing to play, enabled the rebels to judge where the re-inforcements were, so they endeavored to plant their batteries, so as to get a range of the road, their range was an inaccurate one, by double quicking it into the field, we were within the range, the shots and shells whistling over our heads, it was really a splendid sight for a person out of danger. As the rebels changed the position of their artillery, we would be obliged to double-quick it, so as to keep out of their range ; Tower's Brigade had the advance, and several times whilst halting, we would lay down with our arms near us, and endeavor to sleep, but would soon be roused up to change our positions. The cannonnading and musketry was kept up, on both sides, till near mid-night, when Brigadier General Hartsuff, addressed our regiment, saying, " that one of the rebel batteries, had been silenced, and that Brigadier General Ricketts', commanding our Division, wished him to send a regiment to support one of the batteries, and that he had chosen the 'New York Ninth,' for that duty, knowing that if the battery should become engaged, that he would hear a good account of it." The regiment was divided into two wings, each wing supporting a section of artillery ; they laid down some distance from them, but would no sooner get into a doze, then it would be, change position to some other portion of the field, so it was, all night long; at times we were near enough, to hear the rebel officers, giving orders to their men, but the night was so dark, that we could not see each other.

Sunday 10th.—Some time after daybreak, we were relieved from supporting the battery, and returning to the Brigade, we moved into a field of standing corn, where Colonel Stiles again took command of the regiment, having been relieved from his po ition as Military Commander, at Warrenton ; Major Rutherford while in command, behaved gallantly and nobly, proving that he was capable of his assumed position. Throughout the day, both sides were busy burying the dead, a cessation of hostillities having taken place. The day being rainy, the corn stocks was torn up to make a temporary shelter, to protect us from the storm. Towards night, the Brigade moved out of the corn field, into one, with tall, standing grass, and one regiment at a time, was sent after their knapsacks, and returning to the field, pitched their Tents.

Tuesday 12th.—During the morning, broke camp, and laid in the woods near by, and towards night, pitched Tents, on an open field, outside of the woods.

Friday 15th.—In the morning broke camp, and followed in pursuit of the rebels, who had retreated, and crossing the late battle ground, we saw horses laying around unburied, broken wagons scattered round about, and considerable property burnt, having the appearance of a hasty retreat of the rebels ; towards evening, we encamped within two miles of the Rapidan river, on the road leading to it, in an open field ; sent out pickets, about a mile from camp. Made a march of 8 miles.

Since Major General Pope, assumed the command of the "Army of Virginia," besides our knapsacks, blankets, shelter tents, and canteens, we were ordered to carry five days rations in our haversacks, and sixty rounds of cartridges, twenty rounds more, than we had formerly carried, making a heavy load, on a hot, summer's day.

Sunday 17th.—An order having been issued from the War Department, that there should be only one Band to a Brigade, and to muster out all others ; our Band started for home, amidst the regrets of the rank and file of the regiment. Brigadier General Carroll, while reconnoitering the position of the rebels, on the South side of the Rapidan river, was shot at, the ball taken effect in his breast ; he was carried to the rear, in an ambulance, passing our camp at noon. Shortly afterwards, broke camp, and retreated about 2 miles, when we encamped on a level piece of land, and put out pickets.

Monday 18th.—In accordance with an order, issued by President Lincoln, "for a general muster of the Army and Navy of the United States," we were mustered in a field, near camp, by Brigadier General Hartsuff. In the afternoon, striking our tents, and stacking *arms*, laid around till night, when we received orders, to sleep with our *arms*, near us, and equipments on, ready to fall in to line, as quietly as possible. The night was dark, till mid-night, when the moon made his appearance, and we fell quietly into line, and marched a short distance, to the road, where we laid for the remainder of the night; it was pretty chilly, and the troops had kindled fires of rails, all along the road, to keep themselves warm. Our retreat was delayed by the road being filled with the advance troops, and the wagon trains; our corps covered the rear of the whole army.

Tuesday 19th.—About 10 A. M., the road being clear, we continued the retreat, passing through a portion of the late battle field, where was boxes of hard bread, which the rebels had left on their retreat, and which our men pitched upon, with a ravenous and hungry appetite, they being short of rations; pursuing our march, passed through CULPEPPER and BRANDY Station, on a quick march, late in the night, being so dark, that we had to grope our way along; at a late hour, crossed the railroad bridge, over the Rappahannock river, at Rappahannock Station, and moving along its banks for a short distance, the brigade nestled down in a cluster of small pines, in a swampy place, and the men scattered themselves, promiscuously around, to sleep if possible. This was a quick and fatiguing march, of 22 miles.

Wednesday 20th.—In the morning the Brigade getting into shape, the men finding their regiments, moved to higher grounds, near the banks of the river, where the artillery was drawn up in position, and there we formed a *line of battle*, and stacked our *arms*, and laid down in the rear of them. Several times in the day, changed our position, as the rebels were visible on the South side of the river.

Thursday 21st.—Laid in position, on the banks of the river, all day. Our Corps, comprising the Divisions, of King's, Ricketts' and McCalls, were the only troops in the vicinity, which Corps covered the retreat of Pope's Army.

Friday 22d.—Late in the forenoon, our Brigade separating from the Corps, crossed to the South side of the river, about a mile from the railroad bridge, on a *pontoon* bridge, built by the pioneers, of rails ; after crossing, marched within a short distance of the railroad bridge, and encamped in a hollow, near the banks of the river.

Companies were detailed alternately, from each regiment in the Brigade, to throw up earthworks, some distance from camp, working night and day.

Sunday 24th.—It having been raining hard, through the previous day and night, and still continuing, caused the river to raise, and being afraid that the railroad bridge would be carried away, early in the morning, was ordered to cross to the North side of the river, and joining the Division, formed a *line of battle*, near the banks of the river; the rebels took possession of our abandoned earthworks, and shelled us, our artillery returned the compliment, when a fierce cannonading was kept up on both sides for several hours; there was no one injured from our regiment, but several from the Brigade. In the afternoon, continued the retreat, heavy cannonnading being heard in the direction of Sulphur Springs, and near sundown, *bivouac* near the road, in a cluster of pines, and sent out pickets, a short distance; after sundown, a shower of rain passed over, wetting us through. Made a march, of 8 miles.

Monday 25th.—In the morning, resumed the march, on the road leading to Warrenton, the wagon train, taking the road leading to Catlett's Station; the troops pursued their march, passing in sight of WARRENTON, leaving it on our right, and early in the afternoon, encamped on the Waterloo road, the men hungry after a fatiguing march of 12 miles.

Government rations being scarce, our men foraged the country, bringing in hogs, corn, potatoes, etc. ; many an empty stomach, was filled with green corn, roasted with the husks on, and green apples, stewed, which made an apology for a dinner, for a hungry man.

Tuesday 26th.—In the morning, marched about a mile towards Sulphur Springs, having heard cannonnading in that direction, when the Division halted in a field, near the road, for several hours, after which they countermarched, back to their camps.

Wednesday 27th.—In the morning, marched towards Sulphur Springs, about a mile, and after halting for some time, countermarched, back to the camp. Late in the afternoon, made a quick march through WARRENTON, Tower's Brigade, covering the retreat, the roads were rough, and bad, covered with mud and water, and near midnight, halted to rest for awhile, near NEW BALTIMORE, the men laying on the ground to sleep, after a fatiguing march of 8 miles.

Thursday 28th.—About daybreak, took up the line of march, keeping on the road, till within a few miles of GAINESVILLE, when our Division took a short cut across the fields, and came into a road leading to HAYMARKET, where leaving the knapsacks, under a guard, made a

quick march to THOROUGH-FARE GAP, to
hold Longstreet's rebel forces, in check, while the
Union troops were marching to Manassas; our
Division arrived, just in the nick of time, as a few
moments later, Longstreet's forces would have
been through the Gap. Our regiment supported
the Eleventh Pennsylvania, in *line of battle*,
and advanced through tall grass and bushes, and
up a steep and perilous hill; the engagement
was kept up on both sides, with musketry and
artillery, for several hours, keeping them from
coming through the Gap, the required time, when
we withdrawed, the cavalry felling trees across,
as an obstruction. The Eleventh Pennsylvania's,
loss, was severe, our regiment not losing a man.
Returning to Haymarket, and taking up our
knapsacks, made a quick march, and near midnight, *bivouac* near GAINESVILLE; sent out
pickets, and laid down to sleep, after a fatiguing
march of 14 miles.

Friday 29th.—At day-break, marched towards
BRISCOE Station, near which place, early in the
day, we halted for several hours; here the Union
troops were engaged with the rebels, the day
before, compelling the rebels to retreat; resumed
the march, fording Broad Run, and marching to
MANASSAS JUNCTION, where we halted for
some time, and again resuming the march, crossed

the BULL RUN battle-ground, passing a number of log houses, which had been the winter quarters of the rebels, and late in the afternoon, stacked *arms* in a field, near where the Second Battle of BULL RUN, was taking place ; laid down behind the stacks to sleep ; the weather was very chilly. Made a hungry and fatiguing march of 15 miles.

Saturday 30th —Second Battle of Bull Run— Although there had been heavy skirmishing the day previous, it commenced this day in earnest ; Major General McDowell, being in command of the left Flank, sent our Division to different parts of the field, wherever they were needed, for a support, keeping us continually changing positions on the field. Towards noon, we left knapsacks, in the woods, under a guard, and early in the afternoon, our Brigade was placed in the first *line of battle*, advanced through the woods, on to an open field, the rebels plain in sight, and hotly engaged along the line ; here our regiment, which was on the left of the Brigade, double-quicked it, to the extreme left Flank, of the Battle line, and forming in a small cluster of thick woods, laid down in line of battle, waiting for the rebels to advance, through the cleared field ; after a short time, they were seen steadily advancing in column, when within musket range, we opened fire upon them, which caused them to retreat, and we fell back, to a road on the edge of the woods, where we found the Twelfth and Seventeenth, United States, infantry, laying on the road, and our regiment formed to the left of them, being on the extreme left Flank, of the Battle field ; in a short time, the rebel troops, cautiously advanced through the cluster of woods, that we had left, as they came in range, we advanced to the fence, and poured in a deadly volley upon them, and withdrawing from the fence, and loading while laying on our backs, advanced again to the fence, and so on, until we compelled them to fall back ; we must have been engaged nearly two hours, and our loss in killed and wounded was pretty severe ; they having flanked us and placed their artillery, so as to have a cross-fire upon us, poured down their grape and canister in our midst, compelling us to retreat, which we did in good order, and halting in an orchard to the rear, hungry and thirsty. After resting in the orchard for some time, marched a little distance, and halted under a hill, and laid there till after dark, when the Army commenced its famous retreat, in good order, although they were tired and hungry, still they marched along through fear of being taken prisoners ; crossed the Bull Run bridge, and forded Broad Run, and several other streams, and as we neared Centreville, considering ourselves safe from being captured, laid down alongside the road to rest, near morning.

Sunday 31.—Before daybreak, commenced to rain, coming down in torrents, completely drenching us through to the skin, and we completed our retreat to Centreville, where we arrived early in the day, and the different Brigades displayed from high eminences, their colors, so that those who were not able to keep up with their regiments, would find them. The men having been a long time without rations, salt pork and hard bread, was dealt out lavishly. In the afternoon, the Brigade moved out of Centreville, a little distance, where we pitched our Tents, in a low, swampy piece of land. On our retreat from the battle-field, we left our knapsacks behind, which fell into the hands of the rebels, leaving us nothing but our blankets and shelter tents. The retreat commenced after dark, and early the next morning, brought up in CENTREVILLE, a distance of 8 miles.

Monday, September 1st.—Towards noon, made a quick march towards CHANTILLY, distant 4 miles, and there drawing up the Brigade in *line of battle*, across a road, as a support of Kearney's Division, who were engaged with the rebels, both sides keeping up a roar of artillery and musketry, till near sunset, when the contest ceased. Our regiment formed on the left of the road, near a house, and in a field with hay stacked ; stacked *arms*, and laid behind them, all day ; the wounded were carried through our lines, to a house, which was used as a hospital; rained hard all day. At night we took hay from the stack, to lay under us, not being allowed to put up our Tents, or make fires, we laid down in line, our *arms* near us, to sleep, wet and hungry.

Tuesday 2d.—In the morning, were allowed to make fires, to dry our wet tents and blankets, and to cook breakfast with, the rebels having retreated, during the night. About 10 A. M., the Corps made a quick march, passing through FAIRFAX COURT-HOUSE, and taking the road leading to Bailey's Cross Roads, passing through a fertile, and well watered country; the orchards were filled with apples, peaches, etc., which was just beginning to ripen ; and the gardens were filled with vegetables ; several hours after sundown, we encamped on HALL'S HILL, after a laborious march of 20 miles.

Here ends the memorable retreat, of the "Army of Virginia," under Major General Pope, which left the Rapidan river, on the 17th day of August, and pitched their Tents on Hall's Hill, the 2d day of September, having made continuous and laborious marches, with a scarcity of rations, and clothing, many of the men making the marches, barefooted. On our retreat we participated in the engagements at Rappahannock Station, Thoroughfare Gap, Second Bull Run and Chantilly, the nights were very chilly, and the men suffered severely, many of them, not having a shirt to their back.

HALL'S HILL, where we encamped, was about four miles from Alexandria, Va., and the capitol at Washington, could be seen from it, which was six miles, from camp; it was a pleasant and healthy place, not far from the Alexandria and Fairfax railroad.

Our men made themselves as comfortable as possible, receiving the usual government rations, and our accommodating sutler, put up his tent, and opened his goods, which consisted of everything to satiate the appetite.

The "Army of Virginia," were encamped, in the vicinity of UPTON and HALL'S Hills, to rest themselves, and re-organize the Army, after its defeat at Bull Run and Chantilly.

The "Army of Virginia," was re-organized, as the "Army of the Potomac," under command of Major General George B. McClellan; and Major General Joseph Hooker, to command the First Corps, (ours) in place of Major General McDowell, relieved.

Our Corps, comprised the Divisions of King's

Ricketts (ours), and McCall's, Pennsylvania Reserves; and Ricketts' Division, of the Brigades of Tower's, Duryea's and Hartsuff's; and Hartsuff's Brigade, of the Twelfth and Thirteenth Massachusetts, and the Eleventh Pennsylvania, volunteers, and our regiment.

While laying in camp, requisitions were made, for clothing, but they were not drawn.

Fresh beef was drawn every other day, and we recruited ourselves, for the commencement of an active campaign, which took place, after laying in camp, about a week.

From May 29th, to Sept. 6th, 1862, the regiment made twenty-three marches, travelling 234 miles.

CHAPTER VI.

From September 6, to October 26, 1862.

Saturday, September 6th.—The "Army of the Potomac," opened its campaign, under its new commander, by breaking camps, and st rting on a march, about sundown; crossed the Aqueduct Bridge, passing through GEORGETOWN, in the latter part of the night, and pur ued our march, passing through WASHINGTON city, taking the road towards Rockville, and as day was breaking, we halted near the road, a short distance from Washington, and laid down to rest after a toilsome march of 10 miles.

Sunday 7th.—After a few hours rest, fell in to line, and pursued the march, the weather very hot, passed Fort Albany, near Brightswood; along the route, the country was in a high state of cultivation; the orchards filled with apple trees, which hung loaded with that delicious fruit; the fields were filled with potatoes, beans, tomatoes, ect., which were scattered in profusion; towards evening passed through the small village of LEE-BORO, near which, we encamped, having that day marched 11 miles.

Tuesday 9th.—Early in the morning, resumed the march, the sun hot, and the roads dusty; passed through MECHANICS town, late in the evening, near which place, we encamped, in a cleared field, a short distance from the road. Marched through a hot, broiling sun, 10 miles.

Wednesday 10th.—In the morning, wended our way along, passing through COOKESVILLE, near which place, late in the afternoon, we encamped, in a cleared field, near the road, having made a march through the hot sun, of 15 miles.

Friday 12th.—In the afternoon, our regiment received knapsacks, shoes, pants and blankets, but no shirts, or under clothing, when the Brigade took up its line of march, the Sixteenth Maine volunteers, a few days from home, joining our Brigade; passed through LISBON and POPLAR SPRINGS, and near sundown, encamped in RIDGEVILLE, on a cleared field, near the main street. This was a toilsome march of 8 miles.

Saturday 13th.—Early in the morning, resumed the march, leaving the Sixteenth Maine, behind, to guard the railroad; Colonel Stiles, having received a leave of absence, the night previous, the command of the regiment, devolved upon Lieutenant Colonel Atterbury, and the Corps on the march, passed through NEW MARKET, and pursuing the march, long after night fall, crossed the bridge over the Monocacy river, near FREDERICK city, where we encamped, after a tedious march of 13 miles.

Sunday 14th.—Early in the morning broke camp, and took a bye-road that led to Frederick city, halting for some time to allow the troops in advance to push forward, when we resumed the march, passing through the principal streets of the city, where we halted for some time ; the weather was very warm, and on the stoop of nearly every house, sat a bucket of cold water, and fair young maidens, with cups in their hands, filling them, for the soldiers out of the buckets ; in some houses they lavishly gave pies, cakes, etc., to the worn out and hungry soldiers: the glorious " stars and stripes," were proudly floating from many a building, where a week before, they had been pulled down, to make room for the traitors' dirty rag, the "stars and bars," but thanks to the Union cavalry, who several days before, drove the traitors, through the streets, in a hand-to-hand conflict, compelling them to leave the city, when that glorious " old flag," was again re-instated in its former places, amidst the joy and congratulations of the inhabitants, who had been robbed by the rebels, and paid in their worthless currency. Even the little children, welcomed the Union forces, as they were gathered in groups with little flags

in their hands, and waved them, while singing
National "airs," joyfully welcoming us to their
city. All that we met appeared joyous at the re-
occupation of their city, by the Union forces.
Resuming the march, and passing through the
city, took the Middletown pike, the troops marching in column, on both sides of the road, while the
road was filled with artillery; the troops in
advance of our Corps, were engaged with the
rebels, in the streets of Middletown, driving them
through the town; several hours afterwards, as
we marched through that place, we were joyfully
welcomed by the inhabitants, finding a bucket of
cold water, on nearly every stoop, and a young
lady to wait upon us. Marching along, we met
squads of rebel prisoners, going to the rear, under
guard, and passed several barns, filled with them.
We came to a small stream, which we had to ford,
as the rebels had burnt the bridge, on their retreat,
to delay our advance, which they did but slightly,
as the stream was shallow and easily forded.
Our Division on coming near the stream, found
the bridge still burning, and some of the members
of the Fourteenth Brooklyn Militia, of King's
Division, working on an engine, to put out the
fire. After crossing the stream, halted along the
road for some time, the advance troops, engaged a
short distance ahead of us. Resuming our march,

late in the afternoon, left the Hagerstown pike, turning off on a bye-road, where we made a quick march for several miles, halting in a field, unslung knapsacks, and leaving them under guard, pursued the march on quick time, over fields and roads, till we came to SOUTH Mountain, where the battle was being fought; taking the extreme left of the line, the Brigade advanced up the Mountain, over a steep and precipitous road, filled with brush, and small, loose stones, which gave way under our feet; reaching the summit, the brigade formed in *line of battle*, supporting the "Pennsylvania Reserves," belonging to our Corps, who were thrown forward as skirmishers; the engagement was kept up, a long while after dark, when the firing having ceased, the Brigade fell back, a short distance, on a low plain, and supperless, laid down on our *arms*, tired and hungry, after a fatiguing march of 12 miles.

Monday 15th.—Having been allowed to make fires, we cooked our coffee, and the Brigade advanced up the Mountain, our regiment throwing out skirmisher's, to feel for the rebels; after advancing a short distance, news was brought to Major General Hooker, that the rear guard of the rebels, had passed through Boonesboro, at daylight, marching on quick time, and very much scattered, the Union cavalry close at their heels. The Brigade took up the march, descending the Mountain, and halted in a field, near the Hagerstown pike, opposite a tavern, and a few scattered houses, which were deserted, as the occupants had fled, on the approach of the rebels. On account of the road being blocked up with artillery, our wagons, could not reach us, therefore we were compelled to put up with short rations, having issued to us, two crackers, a man, but in the garden, of the tavern, some of the men, found a few vegetables, and on the trees, green apples, which would satiate the appetite. In the vicinity was found, a large number of the rebel's knapsacks, and a great number of their dead, lay unburied, showing that they must have made a hasty retreat. After the road was clear, we pursued the march, passing through SOUTH Mountain Gap, on the road, we met a large number of rebel prisoners, going to the rear, under guard, our cavalry having overtaken the rebels, and captured a large number of them. Passing on through BOONESBORO, the weather being warm, the inhabitants showed their kindness towards us, by supplying us with water, which was found on nearly every stoop, and young ladies to wait upon us. Our country's sacred " Flag," could be seen proudly floating from many a building, and we were gladly welcomed in Boonesboro, as their preservers, from the hordes of traitors, who plundered them, as they passed through the place, on their retreat, several hours before. Taking the road leading to KEEDYS-VILLE, in which place, we halted on the road, for some time; the inhabitants had mostly fled, on the approach of the rebels, whose rear guard, was engaged with our advance troops, a short distance from the town; the cannonading was kept up, till after sundown, when the rebels retreated, and we pursued our march through the town, taking a bye road, and encamping in a field, near Antietam creek, late in the night, hungry, after a march of 12 miles, and nothing to eat.

Tuesday 16th —Drawed rations in the morning, and about 3 P. M., heavy cannonading was heard near by, when we made a quick march, crossing the bridge over Antietam creek, passing through several fields, leaping over stone walls, fences and ditches, under fire of the rebels, seeming incredible that any one, could push through such obstructions, but it was done through the exigencies of the moment; the Division marched through a field of standing corn, laying it low, the shots and shells, whistling over our heads, but we kept on, advancing steadily, till we came within supporting distance of a battery, who had driven a rebel battery from a corn-field, and put theirs in the place of it, when our Brigade laid

down, near the battery, to support it; but some
time after dark, the Division moved into the
woods, near by; it was so dark, that the men
could not see their file leader, therefore being
compelled to hold on to each other, to enable
them to keep their place in the ranks; during our
progress through the woods, many a one, stumbled,
hurting themselves, but not seriously, and after
covering the Brigade, we lay down on our *arms,*
keeping perfectly quiet; several times through the
night, we would be startled from our sleep, by the
firing of the pickets, when rousing up, and grasp-
ing our muskets, stood ready for an attack, if our
pickets were driven in, but the firing ceasing, we
would again lay quietly down to sleep.

Wednesday 17th.—At daybreak, the Brigade
forming in *line of battle*, the left, where our regiment was, advanced through a ploughed field,
under a heavy fire from the rebel artillery; some
of our men were struck with the shells, while
advancing through the field; advanced steadily
along, until we reached a thin strip of woods,
where we came under a heavy musketry fire, the
rebels were in a ploughed field beyond the woods,
near them, was a house burning. in the vicinity of
which, they were pouring a murderous current of
shot and shell upon us, we returned the compliment; there uniform being of the color of the dirt,

we could not see them very well, but we kept them at bay, the battle raged fearfully, men falling on both sides, now, the rebels advancing, and are driven back, then, our troops, advancing and meeting with the same fate, until it is doubtful, who would be the victors, in the end. The roar of artillery, the sharp report of musketry, the officers giving orders, the shouts on making a bayonet charge, and the cheers for re-inforcements, are the attendants of a battle field. Our Brigade having been engaged nearly three hours, and our ammunition expended, we were relieved by troops from Major General Bank's command, and we retired to the rear, our loss being heavy, in killed and wounded. About 5 P. M., the Brigade was again sent to the front, to support a battery on the right Flank, the rebel cavalry, made a *sortie*, but was repulsed by the battery; the firing ceased shortly after sundown, and we remained in a supporting position all night.

When we advanced across the ploughed field, early in the morning, our gallant and brave Brigadier General, George L. Hartsuff, was severely wounded, by a rebel sharpshooter, who was up in a tree; the General was carried off the field, and Colonel Coulter, of the Eleventh Pennsylvania volunteers, assumed command of the Brigade, gallantly leading it into action.

During the engagement, our Corps commander, Major General Joseph Hooker, who also commanded the operations of the Centre, was severely wounded, thereby being compelled to leave the field, before the issue was determined.

The new organization—the Ambulance Corps, worked admirably, it was composed of men detailed from the regiments, some to drive the ambulances, conveying the wounded, a safe distance to the rear, or to the hospitals; and others, as stretcher bearers, to go on the battle field, and carry off the wounded to the ambulances; in the battle of ANTIETAM, they could be seen with the green on their arm, faithfully tending to their duties.

Thursday 18th.—There was but little skirmishing throughout the day, and no regular engagement. We held the same position, as the evening previous, both armies busy, burying their dead, and carrying off the wounded.

Friday 19th.—In the morning, we found the rebels, had made a hasty retreat, crossing the Potomac river, at Shephardstown Ford, in a demoralized condition, their ranks being a great deal thinner, than when they crossed into Maryland. The Brigade was moved to the right of SHARPSBURG, about a mile from the late battle field, where they picketted along the Potomac.

We received our knapsacks, which we had left behind, when we advanced to participate in the battle of SOUTH Mountain.

The water for drinking purposes, had to be carried a long distance, and was very scarce, but there was a nice stream to bathe in, as the weather was pretty warm.

Our Corps commander, Major General Hooker, having been severely wounded, in the late battle, Brigadier General John Reynolds, commanding the " Pennsylvania Reserves," was assigned to the command of the Corps; and Brigadier General Nelson Taylor, of Sickles Brigade, was assigned to the command of our Brigade, in place of Brigadier General Hartsuff, who was wounded during the engagement at Antietam, and promoted Major General.

Friday 26th.—Finding a better position for camp, where the water was more convenient, in the afternoon we moved camp about a mile, near the Potomac river, in the woods, where we picketted along the river, and at which place the Chesapeake and Ohio canal, runs along the river. Drinking water was obtained from springs, issuing from the banks of the river. The weather was dry and cool.

Battallion and Brigade drills, were frequent, on a level field about a mile from camp.

Our Corps was reviewed, on a field, about a mile from Camp, by President Lincoln.

Colonel Stiles, returned from a leave of absence, granted on the march from Ridgeville, and took command of the regiment.

Lieutenant Colonel Atterbury, resigned, he came from home with the regiment, as Captain of company G.; was elected by the Board of Officers, Major, June, '61; was appointed by Governor Morgan, Lieutenant Colonel, Jan., '62; and in the absence of the Colonel, commanded the regiment, at the battles of South Mountain and Antietam.

Major Allan Rutherford, was appointed by Governor Morgan, as Lieutenant Colonel, in place of William Atterbury, resigned; and Captain John Hendrickson, of company G., in place of Allan Rutherford, promoted.

The Sixteenth Maine volunteers, who were left behind, at Ridgeville, to guard the railroad, returned to the Brigade.

Doctor Nordquiest, was detached, as Brigade Surgeon, and Doctor Pinckney, being on detailed duty, the sick of the regiment, was attended to by different doctors, detailed by the Brigade Surgeon.

The Twelfth and Thirteenth Massachusetts volunteers, (of our Brigade) were sent to the Sharpsburg pike, to intercept Stewart's rebel cavalry, on their return, as they had crossed the

Potomac river, into Maryland, at Shephardstown Ford, and was making a raid through Frederick city, but instead of re-crossing the river, at the same place, they re-crossed at Edwards Ferry; and those regiments returned to their camps, without firing a shot.

Adjutant Charles E. Tuthill, resigned, he came from home with the regiment, as Second Lieutenant of company H.; was appointed Adjutant, Sept., 61; and participated in the battles of Cedar Mountain, and Chantilly.

Second Lieutenant Charles E. Strong, of company F., was appointed Adjutant, in place of Charles E. Tuthill, resigned.

Laid encamped in the vicinity of SHARPSBURG, after the battle of ANTIETAM, from the 19th day of September, to the 26th day of October, in which time, we were well fed, and rested. The weather pretty cold, and yet, no under clothing were issued, and a great many, without a shirt to their back.

From Sept. 6th to Oct. 26th, 1862, the regiment made eight marches, travelling 91 miles.

CHAPTER VII.

From October 26, 1862, to April 28, 1863.

Sunday, October 26th.—Early in the morning, struck Tents, and the roads being filled with troops, we remained around camp, till afternoon, the rain pouring down in torrents ; when the roads being clear, our Division proceeded on the march, passing through Sharpsburg, soon after, dark set in, the roads being in a miserable condition, and it raining hard, the men scattered along the road, some, taking shelter in the barns, while others, put up their shelter tents ; but the skeleton of the Division, pursued its march, stumbling along, till about 10 P. M., when they *bivouac* in the woods, the rain descending in torrents. Made a march that day, of 8 miles.

Monday 27th.—The men who had fell out, having reached their regiments, the Division, about 9 A. M., resumed the march, the rain having ceased, passing through CRAMPTON'S Gap, a pass through the South Mountain ; descended into the valley, and encamped in a cleared field, at sundown, near BERKHARDTSVILLE, after marching 8 miles.

Tuesday 28th.—In the morning, resumed the march, the weather fine and clear, and the roads in middling good order; passed through BERKHARDTVILLE, and encamped early in the afternoon, near BERLIN, marching 8 miles.

Thursday 30th.—Early in the morning, took up the line of march, passed through BERLIN, and halted on the banks of the Potomac river, where was two *pontoon* bridges, laid across the river, and the troops and wagon trains, were crossing on them, into Virginia; after several hours, we crossed the bridge, the river here, being about half a mile wide, and landing on the shores of Virginia, marched along the road, passed through LOVETTSVILLE, near which village, early in the day, we encamped, sending out pickets, about two miles from camp. The country was infested with guerillas, who were prowling around the vicinity, before the arrival of our troops. The march was a short and easy one, of 6 miles.

Saturday, November 1st.—Early in the morning, took up the line of march, the weather warm, and clear; passed through the neat, little village of WATERFORD, inhabited by Quakers, their houses were all painted white, presenting a clean and tidy appearance; pursuing our way, passed through a small cluster of houses, known as HAMILTON'S store, and towards sundown, encamped near PERCERVILLE, having made a march of 20 miles.

Sunday 2d—Heard heavy firing throughout the day, and the news was brought that Brigaꝺier General Pleasanton's cavalry, had had an engagement with the rebels at Snickers Gap, a pass in the Blue Ridge Mountain, and that the rebels were defeated, and our troops in possession of the Gap. About midnight, struck Tents, having received orders to be ready to march at a moments notice ; the night was cold, and making large fires, laid down near them, to sleep, not marching that night.

Brigadier General Ricketts', commanding our Division, was assigned to command the "Defences at Harper's Ferry;" he took command, of our Division, June, '62, and and was well liked by the men under his command.

Brigadier General Gibbons, commanding a Brigade in the First Division of the Corps, was assigned to the Second Division, (ours) in place of Brigadier General Ricketts,' relieved.

Monday 3d —After laying with our Tents down, since the mid-night of the day before, about noon, took up our position in the Division, under the new commander, and taking the Aldee pike, passed through SNICKERSVILLE, and long after dark, encamped near that place, having made a quick march of 10 miles.

Tuesday 4th.—Resumed the march in the morning, passing through BLOOMFIELD, near which place, early in the afternoon, we encamped, after a short and easy march of 8 miles.

Wednesday 5th.—In the morning, again took up the line of march, and continued it, for four successive days, encamping at nights, and marching early in the mornings, passing through several small villages.

Sunday 9th.—Continuing the march, passed to the right of WARRENTON, near which, we encamped about noon, in a cluster of woods, the snow falling fast, and the weather very cold. The continuous march since the 5th inst., was 31 miles, over good roads, but the weather was cold and disagreeable.

Tuesday 11th —Late in the day our Brigade was detached from the Division, and marched for Rappahannock Station, under the command of Brigadier General Taylor; after dark, we took the wrong road, and countermarched to the right one, making 8 miles out of the way; the night was a cold and snowy one, and the march fatiguing; pursuing our march, we *bivouac* at midnight, near RAPPAHANNOCK Station, after an irksome march of 16 miles.

Wednesday 12th.—Before daybreak our regiment was sent to the Rappahannock river, about a mile off, to do picket duty, where we remained till about eight o'clock, A. M., when we were relieved by another regiment of the Brigade, and returning, we laid out camp, in a small cluster of woods, a short distance from where we *bivouac* the night previous.

The only troops in the vicinity, were Bayard's Brigade of cavalry, a company of light artillery, and our Brigade, whose duties were to watch the movements of the rebels, on the South side of the river, and to do picket duty, near the river; the artillery placed their cannons in position, so as to command the bridge crossing the river.

Our Brigade was reviewed in a field, near camp, by Brigadier General Bayard, commanding the Brigade of cavalry.

Orders were read on Dress Parade, relieving Major General George B. McClellan, from the command of the "Army of the Potomac," which he assumed in Sept. '62; Major General Ambrose E. Burnsides, commanding the Ninth Army Corps, was appointed his successor.

Several times having received marching orders, struck Tents, and after several hours, the orders being countermanded, the Tents again pitched, and the usual camp duties atttended to.

Lieutenant Colonel Rutherford, resigned; he came from home with the regiment, as Captain of company F.; was appointed by Governor Morgan, as Major, Jan. '62, and commanded the regiment, in the absence of his superior officers, at the battle of Cedar Mountain, where he behaved bravely; he was appointed Lieutenant Colonel, by Governor Morgan, Sept. '62, and participated in all the battles, in which the regiment were engaged, up to the time of his resignation.

Major Hendrickson, was appointed, by Governor Morgan, as Lieutenant Colonel, in place of Allan Rutherford, resigned.

Adjutant Charles E. Strong, resigned; he came from home with the regiment, as a Sergeant in company F., and was elected by his company, as Second Lieutenant, Jan. '62; was appointed Adjutant, Oct. '62; he had participated with the regiment, in all of the battles that they had been engaged in, previous to his resignation.

First Lieutenant Henry P. Clare, of company D., was appointed Adjutant, in place of Charles E. Strong, resigned; Adjutant Clare, came from home with the regiment, as a Sergeant in company D., ; was promoted by Captain Greene, as First Sergeant, Jan. '62; was appointed by Governor Morgan, as First Lieutenant, May '62; and as Adjutant, Nov. '62.

Tuesday 18th.—Towards night, several cavalry regiments, arrived, to burn the bridge, and to cover the rear, on our retreat. About sundown, our Brigade took up the line of march, retreating through BEALTON Station; the night was dark and stormy, and the roads in a miserable condition; some of the teams were stuck in the mud, and with difficulty, were extricated from their perilous position; the march was quick, and fatiguing, so dark, that we could not see where to step; pursued our march till near 10 P. M., when halting, we laid down alongside the road to rest, the rain descending in torrents. We made that night, a quick march of 5 miles.

Wednesday 19th.—Early in the morning, pursued the march, passing through the village of MORRISVILLE, which was entirely deserted, and towards evening, passed SCOTT'S Mills, and crossing the creek, encamped on a hill, near its banks, having made a march of 12 miles, it raining hard all day.

Thursday 20th.—At an early hour in the morning, resumed the march, over muddy roads, and through the rain, and late in the afternoon, encamped within two miles of STAFFORD Court House, some distance from the road, in a cluster of pines. This was a quick and disagreeable march of 10 miles.

Sunday 25th.—In the morning, marched to the road, and took our place in the Division, and marching along for some distance, we took a road, which proved to be the wrong one, when we countermarched about two miles, to the right road, and pursuing the march, encamped early in the day, in an open field, near BROOKS Station, near the Acquia Creek railroad. The march was a quick one of 8 miles.

The camp was badly situated, for wood and water, which had to be carried from a long distance; laying near the railroad, we burnt up the few old ties, that were laying around.

Doctor Nordquiest, detailed as Brigade Surgeon, was detailed by Brigadier General Gibbons, commanding the Division, as Division Surgeon.

The usual camp duties and drills, were attended to, and the Division, was reviewed by its commander.

Wednesday, December 3d.—Moved camp, about half a mile, near a strip of woods, were we were better situated for wood and water.

The Sixteenth Maine and the Twelfth Massachusetts volunteers, were transferred to another Brigade, in the Division, and their place was taken by the Ninety-seventh New York, and Eighty-eighth Pennsylvania volunteers.

We received under-clothing, many of the men having been without them, since the battle of second Bull Run.

Had a very heavy snow storm, and the weather was changeable from wet to dry, and from cold to warm, living in our shelter Tents.

Tuesday 9th.—Early in the morning, broke camp, and marching about 4 miles towards the Rappahannock river, encamped in the woods, early in the day.

Wednesday 10th.—In the morning, resumed the march towards the river, and early in the afternoon, encamped in the woods, within three miles of the Rappahannock river, below Fredericksburg, having marched 5 miles.

Thursday 11th.—Before daybreak, marched out of the woods; and formed the column, on the road, near the edge of the woods, where we laid for some time, and pursuing the march, to within a mile of the river, encamped in the woods. Heavy cannonading was heard, which was ascertained to proceed from the rebels, on the South side of the river, to prevent the Union troops from landing on the South side, in *pontoon* boats, but our troops effected a landing, and drove the rebels from their rifle-pits, and the engineers laid the bridges, for the troops to cross over. About sundown our Division, marched to the river to cross, but the orders were countermanded, and we countermarched about half a mile, and *bivouac* in the woods for the night.

Friday 12th.-Early in the morning, marched to the river, and laid down on its banks, for over an hour, when we crossed the river on a *pontoon* bridge, four miles below Fredericksburg, and halted on the banks for a short time; pursuing the march, and deploying the Thirteenth Massachusetts volunteers, as skirmishers, advanced the Brigade in *line of battle*, cautiously, feeling our way along; advancing about two miles from the *pontoon* bridges, through an open country filled with ditches and swamps, which we managed to wade through, or jump over, we *bivouac* near the Port Royal Road, throwing out the skirmishers of the day, as the pickets for the night, on the other side of the road in a corn field, with the corn stacked; the rebel pickets, were close enough to hold conversation, with our pickets.

Saturday 13th.—Early in the morning, we advanced across the road, into the corn-field, the Thirteenth Massachusetts, deployed as skirmishers, who advanced and fired, while the rebel skirmishers, kept retreating towards a piece of woods, and our line kept advancing steadily, under the command of our brave and gallant Brigadier General, (Taylor) until we neared the woods, when we received a destructive fire of musketry, from the rebels, there secreted, which thinned out our ranks; we returned their fire, and getting nearer the woods, we laid down, using our knapsacks to protect us from a galling fire, which issued from the woods, and also an *enfilading* fire from the artillery, which belched forth its murderous missiles, of shot and shell ; we advanced within a hundred yards of the woods, and kept up a brisk fire, for some time ; the rebel sharpshooters were up in the trees, picking off the officers, and the men fell thick and fast, and were carried off the field, fast as possible, by the brave men of the ambulance corps. Having been under fire for several hours, the Brigade was relieved, and fell back to the river, the engagement was still going on, the battle raging fearfully. The Divisions loss was ascertained to be large, in officers and men, amongst the number was our gallant and brave Division commander, (Brig. Gen. Gibbons) who was severely wounded, and obliged to leave the field. Our regiment's loss was heavy, amongst the number, was the brave and gallant Lieutenant Colonel Hendrickson, who was in command of the regiment, who was severely wounded in the leg, and was carried off the field ; part of the time the regiment was under the command of a Lieutenant. Towards evening the Brigade, again marched to the front, and was put on the reserve, and late in the night, the firing having ceased, we received rations, which we stood greatly in need of. Volunteers from our regiment, went out on the battle-field, with lanterns and stretchers, to bring in all their dead and wounded, that they could find.

Sunday 14th.—Before daylight, our Brigade, moved some distance to the left, still on the reserve ; there was heavy skirmishing kept up, on both sides, nearly all day, but no regular engagement ; at night the firing ceased, and all becoming quiet, at mid-night "the Army," withdrew to the North side of the river, taking up the *pontoon* bridges, and laid near the banks of the river, on the flats, till morning, the rain coming down in torrents.

Monday 15th.—About daybreak, the Brigade marched through the mud and water, into the woods, near by, where we put up our Tents. The rebels having discovered, that we had left them in possession of the South side of the Rappahannock, threw a few shells amongst us, but it did us little or no damage.

Our Division Hospital, was situated near the banks of the river, two miles from where the *pontoon* bridges were laid, and four miles from the battle-field, it was under the supervision of Doctor Nordquiest, who with his assistants, used their utmost endeavors, to make the wounded as comfortable as possible. The wounded were carried in the Ambulances to Falmouth, a distance of three miles, from the Division Hospital, and there, put on the cars, and carried to Acquia creek, and taken from there by steamboats to Washington and Alexandria Hospitals, where they were kindly cared for.

Friday 19th.—The Division took up its line of march, to find winter quarters, the weather was cold and windy, and the march tedious; and late in the day, we halted, and the Brigade encamped near the road, at FLETCHER'S Chapel, where there was a few houses. On the march, the regiment was under the command of Captain Joseph A. Moesch, of company B., who had been in command, since the battle of FREDERICKS-BURG. Our march was a tedious one, of 12 miles.

Our regiment was encamped on a pretty level piece of land, while on the opposite side of the road, lay the rest of the Brigade, on a side hill; the men put up log-houses, to make themselves as comfortable as possible, for the winter.

Brigadier General Robinson, was assigned to the command of the Division, in place of Brigadier General Gibbons, who was severely wounded at the battle of Fredericksburg; he assumed command of the Division, in Nov. '62.

Colonel John W. Stiles, resigned; he came from home, in command of the regiment, and led it, at the battles of Second Bull Run and Chantilly.

Lieutenant Colonel Hendrickson, who was in command of the regiment, at the battle of Fredericksburg, and was wounded in the leg, which was amputated below the knee, was appointed Colonel, in place of John W. Stiles, resigned.

Captain Joseph A. Moesch, of company B., was appointed Lieutenant Colonel, in place of John Hendrickson, promoted.

Captain Dabney W. Diggs, was appointed Major, in place of John Hendrickson, who was promoted Lieutenant Colonel, in Nov. '62.

The men having made themselves comfortable as they supposed, for the winter, and the Brigade built ovens to bake bread in, which was issued to us daily, a loaf of twenty-two ounces, to each one, and potatoes, onions and carrots, with fresh beef, every other day, the men began to take comfort, and to enjoy themselves, from the relaxation of a hard fall campaign, that they had passed through, and the fatigue of their last battle; while enjoying ourselves, the unwelcome news, rang through the camp, "prepare yourselves, for a march," and therefore on the morning of

Wednesday, January 21st., 1863., the Division marched, till late at night, when they *bivouac* near FALMOUTH, after a tedious and disagreeable march of 10 miles.

Thursday 22d.—In the morning, resumed our march towards the Rappahannock river and early in the day, encamped in the woods, within two miles of Banks' Ford, having marched about 4 miles, through a heavy rain storm.

It was the intention of Major General Burnsides, to cross his troops at Banks' Ford, but the *pontoon* train, could not be brought up, as they were stuck in the mud, so also was the artillery, the mud was so deep, that it took an extra number of horses to extricate them.

Friday 23d.—The General, having abandoned the project of crossing the river, which failure was known amongst the troops, as " Burnsides mud march," and as such it will long be remembered, by its participants. The troops laid encamped all day to rest.

Saturday 24th.—In the morning, retraced our way back to our old camp, at FLETCHER'S Chapel, where we arrived late in the day, having marched 12 miles.

The usual camp and picket duties, were attended to, and drilling, when the weather permitted ; and the hours of leisure, were pleasantly spent in playing ball, on the Parade ground, or pitching horse shoes as quoits.

We received a welcome visitor, in the person of Major Hapgood, who had taken the place of Major Sherman, in paying off our regiment, and he paid us four months pay.

Brigadier General Nelson Taylor, commanding our brigade, resigned ; he took command shortly after the battle of Antietam, and was in command of the Brigade, at the battle of Fredericksburg, where he distinguished himself for his bravery and coolness, during action ; he took his departure amidst the regrets of the whole Brigade.

Colonel Leonard, of the Thirteenth Massachusetts volunteers, who was the Senior Colonel of the Brigade, acted as Brigadier General, in place of Nelson Taylor, resigned.

Major General Joseph Hooker, relieved Major General Ambrose E. Burnsides, of the command of the "Army of the Potomac," and reviewed the troops under his command.

One fine morning, we marched about five miles, to a field near BELL Plains, where the Corps was reviewed by President Lincoln.

Doctor Howard Pinckney, resigned ; he came from home with the regiment, as Assistant Surgeon, and in Dec. '61, was detailed in the Army Hospital, at Frederick city, Md., where he remained, until the battle of Antietam, when he took charge of one of the temporary hospitals, on the field, on the breaking up of which, he again returned to the Frederick Hospital, where he remained until he resigned.

The weather during the months of January and February, was very changeable, some days, dry and warm, and others, wet and cold, with several severe snow storms.

When we first encamped, wood was very plentiful, but it soon became scarce, sending the wagons a long distance after it.

The water was good and plenty, and flowed from small rivulets, near by camp.

In the month of March, Major Diggs, resigned; he came from home with the regiment, as private in company C.; was promoted Corporal; discharged by promotion, and was again returned to the regiment, with the appointment of Major, in the month of Nov 1862.

Orders were issued by Major General Hooker, that the men in the different Corps and Divisions, of the "Army of the Potomac, should wear on their hats, in a conspicuous place, a badge denoting the Corps or Division, that they belonged to

The badges to be worn, on all marches, and on all the drills and reviews; the Corps were designated as follows:

First Corps, a Lozenge; Second, a Clover Leaf; Third, a Diamond; Fifth, a Malteese Cross; Sixth, a Roman Cross; Eleventh, a Crescent; Twelfth, a Star.

The Division was designated by the color of the badge, and was as follows :

First Division, Red ; the Second, White ; and the Third, Blue.

In April, we received another visit, from Major Hapgood, who paid us four months pay.

Before closing this chapter, we will say in conclusion, that our regiment, on account of its heavy losses, does not number, but little over two hundred men for active duty.

From Oct. 26th, 1862, to April 28th, 1863, the regiment made nineteen marches, travelling 197 miles.

CHAPTER VIII.

From April 28, to June, 12, 1863.

AFTER laying in winter quarters, for several months, the weather becoming fine, and the spring setting in ; we broke camp, and commenced the spring campaign, on the afternoon of

Tuesday, April 28th., when the Division, took up the line of march, through a drizzling rain storm, towards Falmouth, and late in the evening, encamped in the woods, after a march of 12 miles.

Wednesday 29th.—Before daybreak, marched out of the woods, to the road, a short distance from the woods, where we halted for some time ; pursuing our march for several miles, we halted on the road, a mile from the Rappahannock river, in the forenoon ; and in the afternoon, we went down to the river, near the banks of which, we *bivouac*, on the flats.

The First Division of our Corps, (the First,) under the command of Brigadier General James Wadsworth, crossed the river on a *pontoon* bridge, about four miles below Fredericksburg, in about the same place, where the corps crossed, at the battle of Fredericksburg.

Before the First Division, could cross the river, or the *pontoon* bridges, could be laid, the rebels had to be driven from their rifle-pits; therefore the Fourteenth Brooklyn Militia, and the Twenty-fourth Michigan volunteers, went across the river, in the *pontoon* boats, led by their gallant Division Commander, (Brig. Gen. Wadsworth,) who swam his horse across, the rebels endeavoring to prevent his men, from landing, but having landed, they drove the rebels from the rifle-pits, and taking possession of them, the *pontoons* were laid, when the remainder of the First Division, crossed; leaving the Second and Third, on the North side of the river.

Thursday 30th.—This day was appointed by President Lincoln, as a day of Fasting and prayer, throughout the loyal States, " for the success of our Army and Navy." In the morning, orders were read from Major General Hooker, stating that " our success on the right, exceeded his expectations, that the rebels would have to leave their breastworks, and meet us on our own grounds, or be completely demolished," which news was received with vociferous shouts of applause by the men. In the afternoon, the first Brigade of our Division, formed in a circle, and the Chaplains, exhorted and prayed, and the men sang hymns; soon after the dismissal, the rebels began to shell us, when we fell back to the road, and ensconced ourselves in a long, deep ditch, where we remained all night. The artillery on both sides, kept up an incessant firing, till after sundown, when they having ceased, we settled down to sleep, with our *arms* by our sides, hungry, and weary.

Friday, May 1st.—The day was quiet, no cannonading, and we remained in the ditch.

Saturday 2d.—In the morning, left the ditch, and while preparing for the march, the rebels began to shell us, but double-quicking it, out of range, their well directed missiles, did us no harm; pursuing our march, we passed Falmouth, and was in sight of Fredericksburg, and keeping out of sight of the river, to conceal our movements from the rebels, marched over Corduroy roads, (which are roads built of logs,) and towards night, crossed the river on the *pontoons*, at United States Ford, and encamped a short distance from the banks of the river. We had hardly got through eating supper, when we were ordered to strike Tents, and fall into line, the news having been brought to us, that the Eleventh Corps, had broken, and fell back, while engaged in the battle at CHANCELLORSVILLE, thereby, losing the advantageous position, that we had gained; our Corps, with the exception of the First Division which was left on the South side of the river, marched to the Front, and reached the extreme left of the line, about mid-night, when our regiment was deployed in the woods, as skirmishers, and the rest of the Brigade, cut down trees, and built breastworks, working all night. The day was warm, and the men suffered from the intense heat, the march was a hard and laborious one, of 25 miles.

Sunday 3d.—Cannonading was heard on our right, but none near our Corps. A large number of rebel prisoners, were brought in, who were taken inside of our lines, having been lost in the Wilderness, which was long, thick, continuous woods, reaching for many miles. In the afternoon, we were relieved from the skirmish line, by one of the regiment's in the Brigade, and took their position in the breastworks.

The breastworks was in the Wilderness, on the direct road leading to Fredericksburg, and men were detailed from the regiments in the Brigade, to dig a deep and wide trench, across the road, to prevent the rebel cavalry, from raiding in on us.

The First Division, having re-joined the Corps, took up their position on the left. The operations of the left Flank, was under the command of Major General John Reynolds, commanding the First Corps. (ours)

A number of times, we were called to *arms*, on hearing cannonading and musketry, to the right of us, but we did not fire a shot; the weather set in rainy, filling the trenches, which we had dug behind the breastworks, to lay in, with water.

Trees were cut down, and so arranged, as to make a rather difficult place, for an attack, on our breastworks, and the cannons were so placed, as to mow the rebels down, on their appearance from the woods.

Tuesday 5th.—Late at night, we prepared to cover the retreat of "the Army," across the river, and the Brigade falling in to line, marched out of their intrenchments, to the road, but in moving the artillery, one of their pieces, fell into the deep trench, and was with great difficulty extricated, delaying the march; we returned to our breastworks, where we remained for the night, and the artillery that had moved, returned to their former position, till morning.

Wednesday 6th.—About daybreak, left the breastworks, and taking a path through the woods, for about two miles, came out on a large, level plain, which we found covered with troops, hastening down to cross the river, at Banks' Ford, on the *Pontoon* bridges; we halted a short time, and pursuing the march, crossed the river, and kept on till near sundown, when we encamped in a cleared field, near FALMOUTH, where there was not wood enough, to put up our shelter tents, and were compelled to use our muskets, for that purpose ; the water was poor and a long distance off. It rained throughout the day, and the roads were in a bad condition ; the march was a long and tedious one, of 20 miles.

Thursday 7th.—In the morning, resumed the march, and near sundown, encamped in the woods, near WHITE OAK Church, having marched 8 miles.

The three Brigades of our Division, were reduced to two, on account of the expiration of service, of many of the regiments, and the Second Brigade, comprising the Eleventh, Eighty-eighth and Ninetieth Pennsylania, the Twelfth Massachusetts and the Ninety-seventh New York, and our regiment, were assigned to Brigadier General Baxter.

The Twenty-sixth New York volunteers, on their departure for home, their time having expired, transferred their recruits to our regiment.

The weather becoming warm, and our camping ground in the woods, being unhealthy, we moved camp, on a cleared field, on the edge of the woods, where the water was handier, and the situation healthier ; the weather was very warm and dry, and the drills, were attended to, in the cool part of the day, and the pickets were sent out, about three miles from camp, and the same distance from the Rappahannock river.

The Brigade ovens, were put up, and we had soft bread every day, and carrotts and potatoes, frequently, while we had fresh beef, three times a week, besides, our sutler had a large stock of goods on hand, which were rapidly consumed.

Wednesday, May 27th.—Second Anniversary of the regiment's leaving New York city—was devoted to pleasure and recreation, all drills were laid aside for the day. About 10 A. M., the non-commissioned officers, and privates of the regiment, were drawn up in line, on the Parade ground, and a committee was appointed to wait upon Doctor Nordquiest, and request his attendance; the committee soon returned, bringing the Doctor with them; when Quartermaster Sergeant Toland, presented to Doctor Nordquiest, with an appropriate speech, a splendid gold watch, chain, and key, costing $250, which was the gift of the non-commissioned officers and privates, as a testimonial of his kind care and attention, to their wounded comrades, at the battle of Fredericksburg, while under his charge; the recipient replied in a short, but feeling speech, when the men were dismissed to their quarters, giving three cheers for Doctor Nordquiest. Amongst the visitors at the presentation, was noticed Brigadier General Robinson, commanding the Division, and Brigadier General Baxter, commanding the Brigade, and officers of their staffs, and also several reporters of the New York Journals. We again formed in line, in front of Lieutenant Colonel Moesch's (commanding the regiment,) quarters, when three cheers were given for Brigadier General Robinson; while waiting for a speech from the General, an Orderly came into camp with marching orders, and the General hastily left. Claret Punch was dealt out, by order of Lieutenant Colonel Moesch, when the men returned to their quarters, receiving orders, to strike tents, and be ready to march at a moments notice, but laying in the hot sun, with our tents down for several hours, the orders were countermanded, and the tents again pitched, and the remainder of the day, was given up to pleasant enjoyments.

Received a visit from Major Hapgood, who paid us two months pay.

Colonel Hendrickson, who was wounded in the leg, at the battle of Fredericksburg, visited the regiment, but did not assume command, he was loudly welcomed by the rank and file, as their gallant leader, on that hard fought field, where they lost many of their comrades, who died in the defence of their country.

Lieutenant Colonel Joseph A. Moesch, has been in command of the regiment, since the battle of Fredericksburg, when Colonel Hendrickson, was wounded, he is the only field officer, present, having had no Major, since the resignation of Major Diggs.

Several times received marching orders, and struck Tents, but the orders being countermanded and the tents again pitched, and all the duties attended to as usual.

Surgeon Ketcham, was sent from home, as Assistant Surgeon, in place of Howard Pinckney, resigned, and Doctor Ketcham, was in full medical charge, as the Principal Surgeon, Doctor Nordquiest, was detailed as Division Surgeon.

After returning from the battle of Chancellorsville, we encamped near White Oak Church, for over a month, atending to the usual camp duties.

From April 28th, to June 18th, 1863, the regiment made four marches, travelling 65 miles.

CHAPTER IX.

From June, 12, to July 18, 1863.

Friday, June 12th.—Before daybreak, *reveille* was sounded, and forming Brigade line, about 5 A. M., took up the line of march, passing through a desolate, and poorly watered country; the march was over hills, and through fields, without fences, as the rails had all been burnt up, and over dusty roads, with here, and there, a house, with but slight signs of cultivation around it. Near noon, halted on the road, for an hour or two, to cook dinner, when a volley of musketry was heard, near by; it was ascertained to proceed from the First Division of our Corps, who were executing a sentence of death, upon a deserter, whom they taken from the rebel rifle-pits, below Fredericksburg, when they drove the rebels from them, previous to the battle of Chancellorsville. Resuming the march, passed HARWOOD Church, and crossing a small stream, *bivouac* near its banks, late in the afternoon. The day was warm, and the march was quick, with but few halts, and it was a very fatiguing one, of 22 miles.

Saturday 13th.—Early in the morning, broke camp, and marched through a country, similar to the day previous, but water was scarcer and poorer ; marched slow, and halted often ; a great many of the men's feet were blistered, from the march of the previous day ; in the afternoon, came to BEALTON Station, when we followed the Orange and Alexandria railroad, towards the Rappahannock river, and marching about half a mile, turned into the woods, several hundred yards from the railroad, where late in the afternoon, the Brigade encamped ; another regiment from the Brigade, and ours, was sent out on picket, about a mile from camp, towards the river. The day was clear, but the night was rainy, and the march was a tedious one, of 15 miles.

Sunday 14th.—Early in the morning, returning from picket, we found the Brigade drawn up in line, ready for a march, and taking our position in the Brigade, the column moved towards Bealton Station, and marched along the pike, till we reached Catlett's Station, where we crossed the long railroad bridge, and near which we halted for some time ; pursuing the march, passing over roads, through woods and fields, till about 9 P. M., when we forded a small stream, near BRISCOE Station, and halted in a field, near its banks, to cook supper and rest for awhile ; several hours afterwards, we resumed the march, groping our way along the pike, in the dark, stumbling over the stones and bushes, till after mid-night, when we crossed Broad Run, on pieces of boards and rails, the stream was very narrow, and shallow, and about 5 A. M., we halted near the railroad, in the vicinity of MANASSAS JUNCTION, the men throwing themselves on the ground, tired and sleepy, after marching all day and all night, over rough roads. It was a quick march of 25 miles.

Monday 15th.—After sleeping several hours, we continued the march, through a hot, broiling sun, passing the abandoned earthworks of the rebels, and leaving the railroad, marched across the fields, through a desolate and barren looking country, which was poorly watered, and crossing Bull Run Creek, on logs throwed across for that purpose, and halted in the woods, near its banks, to cook and eat breakfast, where we remained for about an hour, when resuming the march, through a rough and stony country, and early in the afternoon, pitched our Tents, inside of the rebels abandoned breastworks, near CENTREVILLE, having marched 10 miles.

There were several springs of good, clear water, near the camps, and a nice stream to bathe in; the country around was wild and desolate looking, being void of cultivation.

Tuesday 16th.—Towards evening, the members of the regiment, assembled around the quarters of the Lieutenant Colonel, to bid farewell to Colonel Hendrickson, who having his leave of absence, renewed, was going with the sutler, to Alexandria, Va., and from their home; the Colonel made a short, but feeling speech, regretting the necessity of his leaving the regiment, but he hoped that he would soon be able to take command again; he was loudly cheered, and he took his departure, amidst the regrets of the whole regiment, taking home with him, the regiment's STATE COLORS, which were entirely perforated with bullet holes.

Wednesday 17th.—*Reveille* was sounded about 2 A. M., and about daybreak, taking our position in the Brigade, marched through CENTRE-VILLE, and crossing several small and shallow streams, on stones and pieces of rails laid across; the march was through a country, that was under cultivation, the farms looked thrifty, and the fences and dwellings were in good order, but the water was scarce and poor. Our march was through meadows, fields, and woods, over dusty roads, through a hot, broiling sun, and a great many men from our Corps, were sun-struck, and died on the march. In the middle of the afternoon encamped on a cleared field at HERNDON Station, near the Alexandria and Leesburg railroad, seven miles from the latter place. The march was a tedious one, of 15 miles.

We encamped on the estates belonging to the family of the late lamented Captain Herndon, (who was lost on the ill-fated Steamer *Central America*,) and near our encampment was a fine piece of woods, with a running stream of good water, besides several springs. In the vicinity, the battle of Drainesville was fought; the rebels had torn up the track for a long distance towards Leesburg.

Thursday 18th.—*Reveille* sounded 3 A. M., and after eating breakfast, struck Tents, ready to march, but about noon, the orders were countermanded, and the Tents were again pitched, and the usual duties attended to.

Friday 19th.—Early in the morning struck Tents, ready to march, when our regiment received orders, detailing them to guard the Corps wagon train, and we again pitched our Tents, while the rest of the Corps, took up the march. The country in the vicinity of our camp, was infested with guerillas, and we sent pickets out, about half a mile. Towards evening an alarm was created by the report of musketry, when two officers came riding into camp, reporting that they had been fired at, the regiment was put under *arms*, and all becoming quiet, they laid down to spend a disagreeable night, the wind blowing fiercely, and the rain descending in torrents.

Saturday 20th.—*Reveille* sounded at 3 A M., and at 7 A. M., our regiment struck Tents, and marched to the front and rear of the wagon train, to prevent an attack from guerillas; the roads were very muddy; passed through the woods, near the railroad, and near GUILFORD Station, in a splendid pine grove, parked the wagon train, and encamped near by, to guard it. Having made a short march of 4 miles.

GUILFORD Station is situated in Loudon county, on the Alexandria and Leesburg railroad, about five miles from the latter place; it contained a few houses, which were in a delapidated condition, and the few inhabitants that were left, had barely the necessaries of life; the railroad was torn up, to this place.

Our camp was badly situated for water, there being none fit to drink, nearer than a quarter of a mile from camp, in the wells of the houses at Guilford station; and no water to wash in, except a small stream of muddy water, near camp.

Volunteers were sent from the regiment, to Fairfax Station, about twenty miles, to guard the supply train, there and back again; and also foraging parties, were sent out, in the vicinity of camp, after hay and grain.

Early one morning, the regiment leaving their Tents standing, marched about four miles from camp, under direction of the Corps Commander, Major General John Reynolds, who was with us; coming to a piece of woods, we deployed skirmishers, and scoured the woods in search of guerillas, who had been seen lurking around, but finding none, we returned to camp.

Thursday 25th.—About 10 A. M., the wagons proceeding in advance, our regiment marching in the rear, to guard them; passed through a barren and desolate looking country, crossing several small and shallow streams, on pieces of rails, laid across for that purpose; the roads in a muddy and bad condition, and the march slow and tiredsome; the whole army were in advance of us, with the exception of some cavalry, which was in the rear. About 4 P. M , we arrived in sight of the Potomac river, near EDWARD'S FERRY, and parked the wagon train, and the regiment halted, near the banks of the river, the rain pouring down in torrents. About 9 P. M., the troops having all crossed the river, at Edwards Ferry, on the *pontoon* bridges, the wagon train crossed on one of the *pontoons*, while we crossed on the other, and landed on the Maryland shore; the river at this place, is about a mile wide, and the current runs swift. Pursuing our march, passed through fields and swamps, while the wagon train, kept on the road, which was very muddy, and the wagons would get stuck fast, when our regiment would halt, until they were extricated, and then groping our way along in the dark, souse we would go into a mud hole, and feeling our way out, continued the performances at short intervals. About mid-night, passed the village of POOLESVILLE, and near daybreak, halted on the road, near BARNESVILLE, and laid down on the ground to sleep, the rain descending in torrents. Made a slow, but laborious march of 20 miles.

Friday 26th.—After a few hours sleep, the wagon train started, and passing through the village of BARNESVILLE, took a road leading to the Sugar Loaf Mountain; passed around the Mountain, on a very bad road, it rained hard during the time; took the road to GREENFIELD Mills, and passing that place, took another one to ADAMS town, and late in the afternoon, encamped near that place, having marched 15 miles.

Saturday 27th.—Early in the morning, started with the wagon train, and marched to JEFFERSON, there our regiment returned to the Brigade, and marched through MIDDLETOWN, near which place we encamped in the afternoon, having marched 12 miles.

7*

Sunday 28th.—About 3 P. M., taking up the line of march, encamped within a mile of FREDERICK city, about 8 P. M., having made an easy march of 7 miles.

Monday 29th.—Early in the morning, passed through FREDERICK city, and took the Emmittsburg pike, passing through the villages of LEWISTON MECHANICSVILLE, and FRANKLINVILLE, besides other small ones ; passed through a place called the Catoctin Furnace, where there were coal mines ; late in the afternoon passed through EMMITTSBURG, and forming in *line of battle*, on the outskirts of the town, *bivouac* for the night, having made a quick march of 25 miles.

Tuesday 30th.—In the morning, passed through a part of EMMITTSBURG, and crossing the boundary line, between Maryland and Pennsylvania, encamped near the road, having marched 5 miles.

Major General George Meade, assumed command of the " Army of the Potomac," in place of Major General Hooker, relieved.

Wednesday, July 1st.—About 8 A. M., taking up the line of march, on the Emmittsburg pike, to within a few miles of GETTYSBURG, when turning off to the westward of Gettysburg, we took the road leading to Seminary Hill, hearing heavy cannonading and musketry in that direction ;

nearing the hill, we found the First Division of
our Corps, engaged with the rebels, our Division
immediately formed on their right, back of the
town, distant about three miles ; our Corps with
the Third Division, which took its place in line
numbered about 7000 men, and they were arrayed,
against a force, with three times their number, and
were engaged three hours, showing the rebels that
they were not the "raw militia," that they were
led to expect, but the bone and sinew of the " First
Corps, of the Army of the Potomac." After being
engaged for about three hours, taking a large
number of prisoners, and losing about half our
men, the Corps was relieved by a portion of the
Eleventh Corps, and shortly afterwards, the rebels
having outflanked them, all our troops had to fall
back, through the town, to Cemetry Hill, under a
galling fire, and the rebels obtained possession of
the town, having our hospitals in their hands, and
taking a great many of our men prisoners. On
Cemetry Hill, we again formed in line, and our
forces took a new base for operations ; our Division changed positions, a number of times, to keep
out of the range of the rebels artillery, which was
throwing shots and shells, destructively amongst
us ; towards dark, we moved about half a mile to
the left of Cemetry Hill, and after dark we built
breastworks, of stones and rails, to protect us

from the rebel sharpshooters, and Whitworth Gun. Our regiment built breastworks untill a late hour, when we went a short distance in front, on the skirmish line, where we remained for six hours, when we were relieved. This was a fatiguing day's work, fighting, and marching 8 miles.

Major General John Reynolds, commanding our Corps, while gallantly leading his men into action, during the first part of the engagement, was shot by a rebel sharpshooter, in the head; he was carried off the field, but did not live long. His death was not known, till after the Corps was relieved, and created sorrow amongst his men, he was admired for his good character, and for his kind disposition, to the men under his command. General Reynolds was assigned to the command of the First Corps, after the battle of Antietam, and he gallantly led them through the battle of Fredericksburg, where he was noted for his coolness and bravery; and again, at Chancellorsville, where he was put in command of the left wing of the Army; and last, he has fallen at Gettysburg, in defence of his country.

Brigadier General Baxter, commanding our Brigade, had all the officers of his staff, either killed or wounded, while the gallant and brave General, escaped from all harm, coolly riding his charger, at the head of his Brigade.

Thursday 2d.—Heavy cannonading and skirmishing was kept up throughout the day; we changed our position, on whatever part of the line, our services were needed as a support. The water was scarce and poor; and we could not make coffee, as the sharpshooters, were watching their chance to pick off our men. At night, retired a short distance to the rear, and laid on our *arms*.

Friday 3d.—The battle raged fearfully, the rebels endeavoring to drive our troops, from Cemetry Hill, as they held possession of the town; but their attempt proved unsuccessful; our Division marched to the right of the Hill, where we remained for some time, when we double-quicked it, to the left of the Hill, a short distance, and took up our position in the breastworks, vacated by the Second Corps, and at mid-night, our regiment, was sent out on the skirmish line, where we remained for six hours, the rain descending heavily. We were short of rations, and pretty well worn out, with the incessant changes of the past few days.

Saturday 4th.—The rebels evacuated the town, and our troops took possession in the morning, they found the hospitals, as they had left them, the rebels having paroled the wounded, and all that were connected with the hospitals. No cannonading, and but slight skirmishing throughout the day. Remained behind our breastworks, all day, and at midnight, our regiment was sent out on the skirmish line, where we remained for six hours.

Sunday 5th.—At daylight, the skirmishers not seeing the rebels in front of them, they cautiously advanced about a mile, to the edge of a piece of woods, but they found that the rebels had retreated under cover of the night, leaving his dead and wounded behind him. Our Division left the breastworks, and fell back a short distance, to others, vacated by some of our troops, where we drew rations, which had been scarce, since the first days battle, and towards night, we moved out of the breastworks, for a short distance into a cleared field, where we pitched our Tents, for the first time since leaving Emmittsburg, and the men settled down for a comfortable nights rest.

Major General John Newton, was assigned to the command of our Corps, in place of John Reynolds, who was killed in the first days fight, a Gettysburg.

Monday 6th.—Early in the morning, started in pursuit of the rebels, who had retreated towards Maryland ; and we took the road to Emmittsburg, and near sundown, encamped in the field, where we encamped on the march to Gettysburg. This was a quick and rapid march of 8 miles.

Tuesday 7th.—Early in the morning, resuming the march, passed through EMMITTSBURG, and also the small villages of MECHANICSVILLE and LEWISTON; crossed the CATOCSIN Mountain, over a steep and difficult road; the wagons and artillery, were compelled to take another road, as the one that the infantry took, was a mere path, and too precipitous for teams to pass over; about dark, encamped at the foot of the Mountain, in MIDDLETOWN Valley, and sent out a detail from the regiment, to do picket duty, a short distance from the camp. The march was a fatiguing and laborious one, through the rain and mud, a distance of 22 miles.

Wednesday 8th.—At daylight, calling in the picket, we resumed the march, passing through MIDDLETOWN, and halted for several hours, at the foot of SOUTH Mountain, where some of the men, drew shoes, being almost barefooted; resuming the march, crossed SOUTH Mountain pass, and near sundown, halted on the brow of the Mountain, and built breastworks of stones, and laid behind them in *line of battle*; cannonading was heard in the direction of Boonesboro, distant about five miles. The march was a rough one, of 15 miles, through the rain and mud.

Friday 10th.—Early in the morning, took up the line of march, passing through BOONESBORO and BENEVOLA, and near which place, shortly after noon, we halted, and forming in *line of bat-*

tle, threw up breastworks of rails and earth, but near night, we moved further towards the right, about half a mile, and again throwed up breastworks, and laid behind them for the night. The Sixth Corps had a skirmish with the rebels, in the vicinity, and drove them from their position. The day was mild and pleasant, the march was a short one, of 6 miles.

Saturday 11th.—We laid behind our breastworks all day, while the cavalry was a skirmishing with the rebels, and also the Sixth Corps, who drove the rebels from their position.

Sunday 12th.—About noon, started on the pursuit, and passing through FUNKTOWN, which the rebels had evacuated in the morning, crossed the Antietam creek bridge, and halted early in the afternoon, near its banks, on the Hagerstown pike, which place was plainly visible; towards night, marched a short distance to the right of HAGERSTOWN, where we formed in *line of battle*, part of our regiment laying across a dirt road, into a garden, in which was a house, where our General, made his quarters; tearing down the rail and board fences, and the stone walls, we built breastworks of them, across the road, and laid down on our *arms* to rest. A regiment was sent out from the Brigade as skirmishers, when a sharp firing was kept up till after dark.

It rained hard throughout the day and night, and we had little or no shelter. The march was a short one, of 5 miles.

Monday 13th —Heavy skirmishing throughout the day; remained behind our breastworks; there was continual rain.

Tuesday 14th.—In the morning, the skirmishers advancing, found that the rebels had retreated under cover of the night, and towards noon, we started in pursuit of them, passing their abandoned breastworks and rifle-pits, and late in the afternoon, encamped on a hill, near WILLIAMSPORT, having ascertained that the rear guard of the rebels, had in the morning, crossed the river at Williamsport, into Virginia. The march was a quick one, of 8 miles, through the rain.

Wednesday 15th.—At daybreak, marched back to a dirt road, and passing over a portion of the ANTIETAM battle ground, passed through the villages of KEEDYSVILLE and ROHRSVILLE, and late in the afternoon, encamped at the foot of South Mountain, near CRAMPTON'S Gap. It was a quick and rainy march of 18 miles.

Thursday 16th.—In the morning, resuming the march, passed through CRAMPTON'S Gap, and through the village of BERKHARDTSVILLE, and early in the afternoon, encamped near BERLIN, having marched 8 miles.

The march into Pennsylvania and back again, was very continuous, having been in close pursuit of Lee, and his rebel hosts; the men were tired out with continual marching, and some, not able to keep up with their regiments, as the marches were very quick, and there were as many roads, as there were Corps; therefore, the rebels having crossed the river, into Virginia, the troops were encamped, near Berlin, to rest, and for the absentees to join their regiments.

From June 12th, to July 18th, 1863, the regiment made twenty-one marches, travelling 273 miles, and fought in the battle of Gettysburg.

CHAPTER X.

From July 18, to December 4, 1863.

Saturday, July 18th.—At daybreak, took up the line of march, passing through BERLIN, and crossing the Potomac river, on a *pontoon* bridge, into Virginia, and marching on, passed through LOVETTSVILLE and MILLTOWN, and early in the afternoon, encamped, near the neat, little Quaker village of WATERFORD, having marched 12 miles.

Sunday 19th.—At daybreak, resumed the march, passing through the villages of WATERFORD, HARMONY, and HAMILTON, and near the latter place, encamped early in the afternoon, having made a march of 10 miles.

Monday 20th.—On the road again at daybreak, travelling through a hot sun, and passing through the village of MIDDLEBURG, encamped late in the afternoon, on the outskirts of that place, having made a quick and fatiguing march, of 20 miles.

Wednesday 22d.—About sundown, took up the line of march, the night was clear and moonlight, but the roads were rough and stony; pursued our march, till about 3 A. M, when we encamped near WHITE PLAINS, having marched 10 miles.

Thursday 23d.—About 8 A. M., resumed the march, passing through WARRENTON, and outside of the city, late in the afternoon, formed in *line of battle*, expecting an attack from the rebels. The march was a quick one, it raining hard, a part of the time, and it was a fatiguing one, of 12 miles.

Friday 24th.—Men were detailed from each regiment in the Brigade, to throw up earthworks, for protection, working on them, night and day.

Saturday 25th.—Before daybreak, received orders to be ready for a march, and early in the morning, the Division moved ; our regiment was detached from the Brigade, to guard the Corps wagon train, and marched towards WARRENTON JUNCTION, and about 10 A. M., encamped near that place, when our regiment returned to the Brigade, and was drawn up in *line of battle* ; near sundown, we resumed the march, and about 9 P. M., encamped near BEALTON Station, having marched 7 miles from Warrenton Junction, and 9 miles from Warrenton to Warrenton Junction, making a distance of 16 miles.

Monday 27th.—Our regiment was sent two miles towards Warrenton, to do picket duty, for twenty-four hours.

Tuesday 28th.—Our regiment, having been been relieved from picket, returned to camp.

Laid encamped near BEALTON Station, from July 25th, to August 1st, and details were made from the regiments, to build "block houses," and stockades, along the railroad, for its defence

Saturday, August 1st.—Early in the morning, left camp, near Bealton Station, and crossed the Rappahannock river, at Rappahannock Station, on a *pontoon* bridge; and on a hill, near the banks of the river, early in the forenoon, threw up intrenchments, and sent out pickets. The march, was a short one, of 5 miles.

For two days, we were busy throwing up intrenchments, and doing picket duty.

Tuesday 4th.—Formed in *line of battle*, inside of the intrenchments, expecting an attack from the rebel cavalry, which had attacked ours, and were handsomely repulsed, making a rapid retreat.

Saturday 8th.—Moved to another hill, near by, vacated by the Fifth Maryland volunteers, of our Third Division, who had intrenched themselves, Laid out camp, and remained about a week.

Received a visit from Major Hapgood, who paid us two months pay.

Saturday 15th.—About sundown, crossed to the North side of the river, and marched about a mile, when we encamped. Our encampment on the opposite side of the river, was very unhealthy, occasioning a great deal of sickness.

Sunday 16th.—Moved about a quarter of a mile, where we laid out camp, in a beautiful spot, on a side hill, and remained over a week.

Two hundred drafted men and substitutes came from home, to join our regiment, and we again commenced drilling.

Wednesday 26th.—We again moved camp, on a hill, near by, which was a healthier situation.

Colonel Hendrickson, who had been absent on a sick leave, resigned, amidst the regrets of the rank and file of the regiment, by whom he was beloved. He came from home with the regiment, as First Lieutenant of company G., and on the promotion of Captain William Atterbury, to Major, June '61, he was elected by his company, as Captain; appointed by the Governor, as Major, Sept. '62; Lieutenant Colonel, Nov. '62, and was in command of the regiment, at the battle of First Fredericksburg, where he was wounded in the leg, which was amputated below the knee; on the resignation of Colonel Stiles, Jan. '63, he was appointed Colonel, but on account of his wounds, he was unable to take charge of the regiment, therefore, his duties devolved upon Lieutenant Colonel Joseph Moesch.

Sunday, September 13th.—Heavy cannonading was heard in the direction of Culpepper, which was ascertained to be the Second Corps, which had met the rebels, and were holding them in check, untill our lines were established.

Major Hapgood, made us another visit, paying us two months pay.

Wednesday 16th.—About daybreak, crossed to the South side of the Rappahannock river, on a *pontoon* bridge, at Rappahannock Station, and marching along the railroad, passed BRANDY Station, after which, we marched through fields, woods and swamps, and late in the afternoon, halted within three miles of CULPEPPER, where we formed in *line of battle*, on a cleared field, and encamped for the night. The march was a warm, and fatiguing one, of 14 miles.

We laid encamped for several days, doing picket duty, and drilling.

Tuesday 22d.—Received orders, to be ready to march, at a moments notice, with eight days rations, but the order was countermanded, and the usual camp duties and drillings, were attended to, besides a Division Drill, under the command of Brigadier General Robinson.

Thursday 24th.—Our regiment was detached, to guard the Corps wagon train, and we did not break camp, but the rest of the Corps, marched to Raccoon Ford, on the Rapidan river, near which they encamped in *line of battle*, where they remained for several days.

About a hundred drafted men, came from home, to join our regiment, and they were put under drill.

Saturday, October 10th.—In the evening, the " Army of the Potomac,' commenced falling back, and about 9 P. M., our regiment, in charge of the Corps wagon train, took up the march, passing through STEVENSBURG, and crossing to the North side of the Rappahannock river, at Kelly's Ford, marched to BEALTON Station, where we encamped, near noon of the next day, having marched all night, which was very dark, and the roads rough, halting but a few hours to rest. The march was a quick, and fatiguing one, of 20 miles.

Tuesday 13th.—In the morning, took up the line of march, guarding the Corps wagon train, and passing our *line of battle*, at WARRENTON JUNCTION, and pursuing the march, early in the afternoon, halted near WEAVER'S Mills, where we left the wagon train, and joined the Brigade, and pursuing the march, late in the evening, we *bivouac*, near BRISCOE Station, having made a quick and tedious march, of 20 miles.

Wednesday 14th.—At daybreak, resumed the march, sending out skirmishers, on both flanks, expecting an attack from the rebels, at any moment, as our Corps, was in the advance;·

marched along cautiously, and early in the afternoon, halted at CENTREVILLE, and taking up our position, in the rebels abandoned earthworks, we remained for an hour, when receiving orders, we again took up the line of march, and going several miles, halted on the BULL RUN battle ground, and forming in *line of battle*, stacked arms, and remained there for the night. The march, since that morning, was 20 miles.

Thursday 15th.—In the morning, we marched back, two miles towards CENTREVILLE, and encamped on a hill, and sent out pickets. Firing was heard in the direction of Manassas, which was ascertained to proceed from the Second Corps, who were attacked by the rebels, but they were compelled to retreat.

Lieutenant Colonel Moesch, who had been in command of the regiment, since the battle of First Fredericksburg, was appointed Colonel, in place of John Hendrickson, resigned.

William H. Chalmers, was sent from home, by Governor Seymour, to fill the vacancy of Lieutenant Colonel, caused by the promotion of Joseph Moesch, to Colonel.

Captain Henry Williamson, of company L., was appointed Major, in place of Dabney W. Diggs, resigned, the previous winter.

Monday 19th.—Early in the morning, taking up the line of march, passed through GAINESVILLE and HAYMARKET, and near the latter place, late in the afternoon, we *bivouac*. The day was rainy, and the march was a fatiguing one, of 8 miles. The night was cold and damp.

Tuesday 20th.—About 2 P. M., resuming the march, passed through THOROUGH-FARE Gap, a pass in the Blue Ridge Mountain, after dark; and fording a small stream, that lay across the road, we encamped about a mile from the Gap, forming in *line of battle*, and stacking *arms*, for the night, having marched 6 miles. The night was cold, and the men were chilly, after fording the stream, that laid across the road.

Saturday 24th.—Early in the morning, marched back through the Gap, and passing through HAYMARKET and GAINESVILLE, and fording several creeks, the water being pretty deep, and the rain pouring down in torrents; proceeding on the march, we halted about 9 P. M., at BRISCOE Station, and forming in *line of battle*, remained there, for the night, having marched 15 miles.

Laid out camp, and attended to the usual duties of picket and drilling, and remained nearly a fortnight.

Thursday, November 5th.— About 4 P. M. taking up the line of march, encamped after dark, near CATLETT'S Station, having made a march of 6 miles, through the rain.

Saturday 7th.—After daybreak, again took up the line of march, passing WARRENTON JUNCTION, and through the small village of MORRISVILLE, and leaving Bealton Station, on our right, encamped early in the day, near Kelley's Ford, on the Rappahannock river, having made a march of 7 miles.

Sunday 8th.—At daybreak, resumed the march, crossing the Rappahannock river, on a *pontoon* bridge, at Kelleys Ford, and pursuing the march, encamped late in the afternoon, near BRANDY Station, formed in *line of battle*, and remained for the night, having marched 10 miles.

Monday 9th.—In the afternoon, marched from Brandy Station, and re-crossed the Rappahannock river, on a *pontoon* bridge, at Rappahannock Station, and marching to BEALTON Station, where the Eleventh Pennsylvania volunteers, and our regiment, were detached from the Brigade, and taking the road towards Warrenton, we *bivouac* near LIBERTY, about 10 P. M., the snow falling fast. The march was a cold one, of 12 miles.

Tuesday 10th.—Laid out camp, and attended to drilling and picket duties, besides which, details were sent from the regiment, to repair the railroad, which the rebels had destroyed.

Saturday 21st.—Our pickets were surprised, by a squadron of rebel cavalry, dressed in our uniform, who drove in our pickets, captured some of the hospital stores and wagons, and took some of our men, prisoners, when they retired; we re-established the lines, and strengthened the pickets.

Monday 23d.—At daybreak, the Eleventh Pennsylvania volunteers, and our regiment, returned to BEALTON Station, and halted about an hour, for the Division to come up, on which we marched to within two miles of RAPPAHANNOCK Station, where we encamped early in the day, having marched 5 miles.

Tuesday 24th.—In the morning, received orders to strike Tents, and fall into line, ready to march; but shortly afterwards, the orders were countermanded, and the Tents were again pitched.

Thursday 26th.—Early in the morning, taking up the line of march, crossed to the South side of the Rappahannock river, on a *pontoon* bridge, at Rappahannock Station, and passing through the small village of RICHARDSVILLE, we halted about an hour, when pursuing the march, crossed the Rapidan river, on a *pontoon* bridge, at Culpepper Mine Ford, and marching about a mile from the river, encamped late at night, near the gold mines, which had previous to the rebellion, been very productive, but since, they had not been worked. This was a very long and wearysome march, of 15 miles, and the sound of cannonading was heard in the direction, that we were marching, there being troops in advance of us.

Friday 27th.—At daybreak, resumed the march, passing through the Wilderness, on the edge of which. we formed in *line of battle*, late in the afternoon, and there, remained for the night. Cannonading was heard in the direction, that we were marching. We marched that day 15 miles.

Saturday 28th.—At daybreak, marched about two miles, and formed in *line of battle*, on the left of the Second Corps, the line gradually advanced, the rebels falling back ; we advanced about two miles, and halted on a ridge of hills, near MINE Run, for the night, having marched 4 miles.

Sunday 29th.—Major General Meade, accompanied by some English officers, rode along the lines, taking a view of the rebels, who laid behind formidable breastworks, in front of our army. We did not change our position, throughout the day. Rained all day.

Monday 30th.—At daybreak, marched about a mile further to the right, and again formed in *line of battle* ; there was cannonading and skirmishing along the lines, this, and the day before, but our Division did not become engaged.

Tuesday, December 1st.—About 4 P. M., we

marched in retreat, and passing Robertson's Tavern, and after dark, we encamped near Germania Ford, and our regiment was sent out a short distance, on picket. The march was a quick one, of 8 miles.

Wednesday 2d.—Early in the morning, our Brigade only, crossed the Rapidan river, on a *pontoon* bridge, at Germania Ford, and formed in *line of battle*, near the banks of the river, where we remained for several hours; pursuing the march, we encamped late at night, near BRANDY Station, having marched 10 miles.

Thursday 3d.—Early in the morning, resumed the march, with the Division, and *forded* the Rappahannock river, at Kelly's Ford, and late in the afternoon, encamped about half a mile, from the Ford, and our regiment was sent out a short distance on picket. We made a march that day, of 14 miles.

Friday 4th.—About 10 A. M., *re-forded* the river, at Kelly's Ford, and encamped on the South side of the river, about a mile from its banks. The object in *fording* the river, twice in twenty-four hours, through the dead of winter, was a mystery that remained unexplained to the men; but the supposition was, that it was the ebulition of angry feelings, from the one, that ordered it. However, it was uncalled for.

Having encamped in the woods, the men cut down the trees, to build log houses for their winter quarters, the drills were dispensed with, and the men set themselves industriously to work, to finish their houses, which they covered with their shelter tents, making themselves quite comfortable, for the cold weather.

Several times received marching orders, but they were countermanded, and the house building went on, and the pickets were sent out.

From July 18th, to December 24th, 1863, the regiment made twenty-five marches, travelling a distance of 294 miles.

CHAPTER XI.

From December 24, 1863, to May 4, 1864.

GETTING our log-houses about finished, and beginning to get comfortably settled for the winter, not expecting to move again till spring, and after being encamped about three weeks, at daybreak, in the morning of

Thursday, December 24th., we prepared for the march, and taking our position in the Brigade marched through CULPEPPER, and followed the railroad, and encamped late in the afternoon, in a low, swampy, piece of woods, near MITCHELL'S Station, having marched 15 miles.

Laid out camp, and christened it, the "Mud Hole," as we could not move, without getting knee-deep, into that plastic article. The weather was cold and disagreeable, and picketing was attended to. We remained in this "slough of despond," till the first day of the new year.

Friday, January 1st, 1864.—On this opening of a New Year, while our friends in the Empire State, are comfortably enjoying themselves, making and receiving *New Years' calls*, we received a *call*, to leave the "mud hole," and march, which we did, following the railroad for a couple of miles, when we encamped on a hill, in the woods, near a splendid creek, where we commenced to build winter quarters, for the second time.

Saturday 2d.—Our labors of building winter quarters, ceased, as we again commenced the march, about 2 P. M., and marching about a mile, halted for several hours, when pursuing the march about a mile further, encamped at night, in the woods, near CEDAR Mountain, and sent out pickets. The march was a short one, of 3 miles.

For the third time, commenced building winter quarters; the weather was very severe, had had several very heavy snow storms, and considerable wet weather.

The Reverend Mr. Roe, was sent from home, as Chaplain, to the regiment, having been without one, since the resignation of Chaplain Phillips, in January, 1863.

Our Brigade, being encamped in the advance, acted as a reserve for the pickets, and being within supporting distance, kept our *arms* stacked, prepared for a sudden attack, with orders in case of a retreat, to burn everything, leaving nothing behind for the rebels use.

Tuesday 5th.—The Eighty-eighth and Ninetieth Pennsylvania, and the Twelfth Massachusetts volunteers, were detached from the Brigade and marched to Culpepper. The rest of the Brigade, received marching orders, but they were countermanded.

We remained encamped, doing picket duty, and were very comfortable in our log-houses. as we supposed for the remainder of the winter, but we were disappointed in our expectations, for after, being encamped, nearly a month, the remainder of our Brigade, took up the line of march, at 4 o'clock, on the morning of

Friday 29th., and marched to CULPEPPER, which place we reached about 10 A. M., and quartered in the houses, for the remainder of that day and night, having made a march of 8 miles.

Saturday 30th.—In the morning, passed through CULPEPPER, taking the Sperryville pike, and halted in the woods, near the road, about two miles from Culpepper, here we found the regiments, that had left the Brigade, at Cedar Mountain, snugly ensconced in their winter quarters, and joining the Brigade, we again, for the *fourth* time, cut logs, and commenced building our winter quarters, and covering them with the shelter tents.

We again, finished our houses, and was making ourselves comfortable, till spring, when we were roused from our sleep, at 1 A. M.,

Saturday, February 6th, and at daybreak, we were on the road, and marching towards the Rapidan river, halted near Raccoon Ford, early in the afternoon, and forming in *line of battle, bivouac* for the night, having marched 12 miles, through the rain and cold. Firing was heard to our left, on the opposite side of the Rapidan river, and was continued long after dark ; when some of our troops that were across the river, were compelled to re-cross.

Sunday 7th.—At daybreak, marched in retreat, and halted in the woods for several hours, to allow the artillery to take the advance, when marching about two miles, halted in a field, where we laid till near sundown ; when again, resuming the march, passed through CULPEPPER, and taking the Sperryville pike, returned to the camp, that we had left the day before, which we reached about 10 P. M., having marched 12 miles through the mud.

Monday 15th.—Marched to a level plain, near Culpepper, where the First Corps, (ours) was reviewed by Major, General Sedgewick, of the Sixth Corps, who was in command of the "Army of the Potomac," during the absence of Major General Meade.

Monday 22.—Washington's birth-day. Our Division marched to a level plain, near Culpepper,

where we were reviewed by Major General
Sedgewick, acting Commander, of the Army, and
Brigadier General Robinson, commanding the
Division.

Tuesday 23d.—In the morning, marched two
miles beyond Culpepper, where on a level plain,
our Corps, with its artillery, was reviewed by
Major General Newton, commanding the Corps.

Details were made from each regiment, in the
Brigade, as a guard for the signal station, on
Cedar Mountain.

The Brigade, sent details from each regiment,
to do picket duty, near Mitchell's Station, where
they were carried in the cars, a distance from
camp, of 8 miles; and also picketed on the Sperryville road, several miles from the camp.

Monday 29th.—In the morning, the Corps was
reviewed, on the level plain, near Culpepper, by
Lieutenant General Grant; during the review, it
commenced to rain, when the troops were dismissed, and returned to camp.

Orders were issued from the War Department,
offering those, who had served two years, and
over, strong inducements to re-enlist, granting
them a thirty days furlough, and extra bounty
money. Nearly all of the Eleventh and Eighty-
eighth Pennsylvania volunteers, re-enlisted, and
went home, also about twenty from our regiment,

and a large number from the other regiments, throughout the Armies.

We received fresh bread daily, from Alexandria, Va., and fresh meat and vegetables, such as carrotts, potatoes and turnips, were issued pretty often, and rations were plenty.

Friday, March 25th.—Orders were issued by Major General Meade, that his Army, would be temporarily consolidated into three Corps, but would still retain their Corps Badges; the First Corps, (ours) would be merged into the Fifth, and would be under the command of Major General Warren; the Third, into the Second, under Major General Hancock, and one Division of the Third, into the Sixth, under command of Major General Sedgewick. We retained our Division and Brigade commanders, and was designated, as the Second Division of the Fifth Army Corps.

Major Hapgood, once more made us a friendly visit, with two months pay.

MARCH, was a cold, rainy and disagreeable month, we had several snow storms, and considerable wet weather, during this month.

APRIL, was ushered in, with a snow storm, and during the month, there was a great deal of rainy weather.

The Maryland regiments, of our Division, having gone home to vote, details were sent out from our Brigade, to do picket duty, on Pony Mountain, seven miles beyond Culpepper, until their return, which was about a fortnight.

Orders were issued from the War Department, transferring seaman, from the Army to the Navy ; about thirty, were transferred from our regiment.

The regiments that had gone home, from the Brigade to re-enlist, returned, and the Ninetieth Pennsylvania volunteers, was transferred to the First Brigade, at Mitchell's Station, to take the place of the One hundred and Seventh Pennsylvania volunteers, which had gone home to re-enlist.

The weather becoming settled, and spring having made its appearance, preparations were made for opening the campaign ; clothing and new shelter tents were issued ; all civilians and sutlers, were ordered to the rear ; officers and men were ordered to reduce their baggage ; and the pioneer Corps, composed of details, from the different regiments in the Brigade, were moved to Brigade Quarters.

Orders were issued to drill with knapsacks; having company drills, in the morning, in the fields, around camp ; Brigade and Battallion drills, in the afternoon of every alternate day, on the level plain, near Culpepper ; and target shooting, at least, once a week, on the fields, near camp, where there was pretty accurate firing.

Major General Meade's Head Quarter's, had been at Brandy Station, all winter, but on the opening of the spring, it was removed to Culpepper, where Lieutenant General Grant, and also Major General Warren, established their quarters.

Details were made from some of the regiments, but none from ours, to throw ap rifle-pits, near Culpepper.

No civilians or soldiers, outside of Culpepper, could visit the city, without a pass from a Brigadier or Major General.

In closing this chapter, we close the winter, wherein, we forded the Rappahannock river, twice, and built winter quarters, four times. The next chapter, will open the spring campaign, after being encamped, near Culpepper, about three months, doing picket, and the usual duties.

From December 24th, 1863, to May 3d, 1864 the regiment made five marches, travelling a distance of 52 miles.

CHAPTER XII.

From May 3, to June 12, 1864.

Tuesday 3d. After *tattoo* had beat, orders were received to pack up, and be ready to march, at ten o'clock, that night, and whatever was left behind, to destroy, to prevent it, from falling into the hands of the rebels ; but were ordered not to makes any fires, which would disclose our movements ; the men, were to have eight days rations, and fifty rounds of ammunition. The arrangements being all completed, we marched quietly out of our camp at *mid-night*, and took up our position in the Brigade, on the road, where the Division formed ; the night was dark, and our march laid through fields and swamps, leaping ditches, plunging into small pools of mud and water, and stumbling over stones and brushes, that lay in the way ; passed by PONY Mountain, crossing the fields, and marching over narrow roads, we passed through the small village of STEVENSBURG, about daylight,

Wednesday 4th., and marched rapidly along, over rough and stony roads, until we came to a piece of woods, with a plank road running through it, which road we took, and marching about two miles, we came to a cleared field, and halted there to cook and eat breakfast, where we remained about an hour, and pursuing the march, along the plank road, for about a quarter of a mile, when we came to another piece of woods, and marching through it, for about a mile, came to another cleared field, and crossing it, for about half a mile, came to Germania Ford, on the Rapidan river, and crossing it, on a *pontoon* bridge of six boats, (the river was not more than thirty yards wide at this Ford,) halted near the banks of the river, for several hours. On both sides of the river, the land is high and undulating; on the South side, the rebels, had throwed up formidable earthworks and rifle-pits, for a long distance, which they had abandoned. About noon, pursuing our march, along the Fredericksburg Plank road, which passes through the *Wilderness*, and sending company C., out on our Flanks, as skirmishers, to protect and give notice of danger; we cautiously advanced, till about 4 P. M., when turning off the road, into the woods, formed in *line of battle*, and stacking *arms*, pitched Tents, for the night, and sent out a Brigade guard. The weather was very warm, and the roads dusty; the march was quick, and the halts not frequent, and of short duration; it was a fatiguing march of 16 miles.

Thursday 5th.—Before daylight, turned out, and eat breakfast, and about daylight, marched to the road, and formed in Division line, the left to the front, and throwing out company H., on the Flanks, as skirmishers, we marched about a mile, and halted ; we heard firing, in the vicinity, which was ascertained, to proceed from the Fourth Division of our Corps, (the Fifth,) whose skirmishers had met the rebels, in the *Wilderness*, and was endeavoring to check their advance ; resuming the march after a short time, we passed through a small cluster of woods, and formed in *line of battle*, behind breastworks, to support the artillery which was placed in position, and was dealing out its leaden missiles, to the discomfiture of the rebels; in front of us, was a cleared field, and a few hundred yards, was a piece of woods, where the rebels lay ; the Union troops advanced some distance into the woods, when a hot, and sharp, contest with musketry ensued, laying many a poor fellow, low ; we could not use our artillery, as there would be danger of injuring our own men, who were hotly engaged in the woods. After remaining as a support for the artillery for some time, the Brigade, was withdrawn some distance, to a side hill, ready to re-inforce any part of the lines, wherever it was deemed necessary ; there we remained until, about 5 P· M., when we were sent to re-inforce the Sixth Corps, we advanced in *line of batle*, over an open field, across a deep ditch, whose banks were very steep, and entered the *Wilderness*, where the battle was raging ; our regiment, was in the second *line of battle*, but part of our Brigade was in the first line; we advanced through thick underbrush, for some distance, when we halted ; soon, the rebels, who could not be seen any distance, through the thick woods, simultaneously poured a volley into our first line, which caused it, to break, and they fell back on the second, but soon rallying, they again formed in line, and drove the rebels some distance, and long after dark, the firing having ceased, we laid down on our *arms*, to rest from a fatiguing day's work. We lost heavily in killed and wounded, which were carried off the field, during the night, to their respective Division Hospital Tents, all of which where several miles from the battle-field.

Friday 6th.—The battle raged all day, driving the rebels slowly before us. Our loss was heavy, in killed and wounded, amongst the officers and men ; among the number killed was our Colonel, Joseph Moesch, who was shot, while gallantly leading, the regiment into action ; his body was carried to our Division Hospital, where some boards were obtained, with great difficulty, and made into a coffin, and Chaplain Roe, attended to his burial, near the hospital. Colonel Moesch came from home with the regiment, as Sergeant in company B., and was elected by his company, as Captain, Jan '62, and was in command of the regiment, after the battle of First Fredericksburg, and was promoted Lieutenant Colonel, Jan. '63, still, in command of the regiment, and leading them with honor, at the battle of Chancellorsville; he was promoted Colonel, Oct. '63, and was killed, in defending his country's rights; one, among the number, who has shed his blood, for the cause of Freedom and Liberty.

Among the wounded of the second day's battle, was our brave Brigadier General Baxter, who was severely wounded, and carried off the field, his duties devolving upon Colonel Coulter, of the Eleventh Pennsylvania volunteers, who faithfully discharged them. General Baxter, assumed command of our Brigade, after the battle of Chancellorsville, and in the battle of Gettysburg, coolly and bravely, led his Brigade, wherever its aid was needed, losing every one of his staff Officers, while he was spared to bleed for his country, in the battles of the *Wilderness*, where he was severely, not dangerously wounded; he was one of the brave sons of Michigan, of whom she may be justly proud, and led the *forlorn* hope, at the battle of First Fredericksburg, when Colonel of a regiment.

Saturday 7th.—We arose at 3 A. M., after laying on the battle-field all night, and marched to the right of the line, a distance of 3 miles, and there intrenched ourselves; about 4 P. M. our Division was relieved, and then marched on the Fredericksburg Plank road, to within half a mile of the Rapidan river, and halted near sundown, having marched 7 miles. About an hour after sundown, marched back to the extreme right, a distance of 9 miles, and halted an hour before daybreak. The distance marched that day, was 19 miles.

Sunday 8th.—At daybreak, we charged the breastworks, of a body of rebel cavalry, and drove them about three miles, when they led us into an ambuscade of Longstreet's Corps; our Division charged *in mass*, and was repulsed, when two other Divisions of our Corps, charged the works, and were repulsed. The Corps being scattered, we fell back about two mile, and threw up breastworks, and re-organized the Corps; there we remained until about 6 P. M., when hearing firing to our right, we advanced to re-inforce the Sixth Corps, but they having driven the rebels, our services, were not needed, and we remained in the rear of the Sixth Corps, as a reserve. In the charge, made in the morning, Brigadier General Robinson, commanding our Division, was severely wounded, and was carried off the field, and his command, was assigned to Brigadier General Crawford. General Robinson, was placed in command of our Division, after the battle of First Fredericksburg.

Monday 9th.—Intrenched ourselves, and supported two lines of battle, when the skirmishers advanced, and a general engagement took place, which ended in the repulse of the rebels.

Tuesday 10th.—Throughout the morning, there was heavy skirmishing, and the right centre, swung round, driving the rebels from their position, which was an advantageous one, for our artillery, which was placed on an eminence, and done good execution. About noon, our regiment, advanced by the Flank, and formed in *line of battle,* on the left of the Brigade ; the right wing advanced, and met the rebels on the top of a hill, when an engagement took place, which was kept up for some time, and being repulsed, we laid in line, in the rear of the Second Corps, until the contest was renewed, when we attempted to drive the rebels from their breastworks, but they drove us from the hill, and we fell back into our intrenchments, where we remained for the night.

Thursday 12th.—About 10 A. M., we advanced on the rebels breastworks, where our loss was heavy, and we were relieved early in the afternoon, and returned to our intrenchments ; and our regiment was sent out towards night, to do picket duty.

Friday 13th.—Our regiment was relieved from picket duty, early in the morning, and returning to the intrenchments, there remained till we took up the line of march at mid-night, and taking the Fredericksburg pike, which was very muddy, we reached the extreme left, a distance of 7 miles, about daybreak, on the morning of

Saturday 14th., and in the afternoon advanced in *line of battle*, along a brook, near the edge of the woods, where the rebels were in position, who had attacked our Signal Corps, which was supported by two regiments of infantry, and were compelled to fall back, when the rebels opened their batteries upon our Corps, shelling us briskly for some time, with but little effect. Our artillery on the left, opened a fire upon the rebels, which compelled them to fall back, leaving us in possession of the field, and throwing up breastworks, where we remained for several days, there being nothing but light skirmishing, during that time.

Tuesday 17th.—About dusk, our Corps moved about a mile to the front, and threw up breastworks, and *bivouac* for the night.

Wednesday 18th.—The rebels opened a murderous fire of shot and shell, upon us, which did us but little damage; we remained behind the breastworks, till evening, when our regiment was sent out on picket, and during the night, while visiting the picket line, Colonel Coulter, of the Eleventh Pennsylania volunteers, commanding our Brigade, was shot at, and severely wounded; and his command devolved upon Colonel Bates, of the Twelfth Massachusetts volunteers.

Thursday 19th.—Our regiment was relieved from picket, and marched to the right, where we found some of our troops hotly engaged with a part of Ewell's Corps, which were repulsed with great slaughter. Our Brigade was not engaged in the contest, but supported the Heavy Artillery Brigade, (which was doing infantry duty.)

Saturday 21st.—About 11 A. M., resumed the march, and going about 9 miles came to the Mattapony river, and crossing it, advanced in *line of battle*, about a mile, driving the foe before us ; and then halted and *bivouac* for the night.

Sunday 22d. —About daylight, the Brigade advanced in *line of battle*, to *reconnoitre* the rebels position, and after advancing about two miles, we came across their cavalry, which being on the retreat, we returned back to the Division, and taking up the line of march on the Hanover Junction pike road, marched about 8 miles, and at sundown, *bivouac* for the night. Marched that day, about 10 miles.

Monday 23d.—At daylight resumed our march on the Hanover Junction pike road, and late in the afternoon, forded the North Anna river, and found the rebels in force, in our front. We formed on the heights in *line of battle*, and our foe opened their Artillery upon us, about dark, which after a little delay, was replied to by our batteries, and a lively infantry skirmish took place, which was contined to a late hour. The loss on our side was but slight, and we laid down to rest, having marched that day, 12 miles.

Tuesday 24th.—The rebels having fell back, during the night, we marched in pursuit of them, and proceeding several miles, we found them strongly intrenched on the edge of a dense piece of woods. Forming in *line of battle*, and sending out skirmishers, we threw up breastworks, and towards night, our regiment was sent out as a support, and returned to the Brigade, the next morning.

Thursday 26th.—Late in the night, we quietly left our breastworks, and after several hours delay, we re-crossed the North Anna river, long before daybreak of the next morning, and marching several miles further, halted and drew rations, and continuing the march, *bivouac* after dark on the night of *Friday* the 27th., near Reedy creek, after a hard march of 18 miles.

Saturday 28th.—Early in the morning, resuming the march, passed through the village of MAN-GOHICK, and crossing the Pamunkey river, early in the afternoon, formed in *line of battle*, a short distance from the banks of that river, and threw up breastworks in *echelon* by regiments, where we remained for the night, having marched 10 miles.

Sunday 29th.—Leaving our breastworks in the morning, we marched about two miles, towards the left, when halting for several hours, we again marched towards the front, about two miles, and halting, threw up breastworks, but near dark, we marched about two miles to the rear, where we *bivouac*, having made three marches of 6 miles.

Monday 30th.—Late in the afternoon, marched to the front, there being heavy skirmishing and artillery firing going on. Our Division which had been separated for some time, were re-organized under the command of Brigadier General Lockwood, and remained in the front all night.

Tuesday 31st.—Heavy firing on the right; the Union troops, scattering the rebel forces in every direction; our Division were not engaged, but laid quiet all day.

Wednesday, June 1st.—Swung our left around, about a mile, and about 10 A. M., our regiment was sent out on the skirmish line, when heavy skirmishing took place, and the rebels shelled us fearfully, causing a heavy loss in our regiment. After sundown, we were relieved from the skirmish line, and marched to join our Brigade, which had moved about a mile to the left, and we were kept as a reserve picket all night.

Thursday 2d. Relieved the right wing, early in the morning, and was on the skirmish line, until early in the afternoon of

Friday 3d., when we were relieved, and joined the Brigade, late in the afternoon, when a heavy engagement, took place on the right, which lasted for over an hour, when a heavy artillery fire took place, which was kept up briskly for some time, by both sides. Threw up breastworks, and laid behind them all night.

Sunday 5th.— Leaving our breastworks, we marched to the right, nearly a mile, and halted till within an hour of midnight, when we marched to the left, about 5 miles, passing GAINES Mills, and towards morning, we *bivouac* near that place.

Tuesday 7th.—Received orders from Corps Head-Quarters, to report in New York city, for muster-out, and the regiment left the front, about 5 P. M , with 87 men, and 20 officers, after transferring those whose term of service had not expired, to the 97th New York volunteers; and proceeding on their way, they reached White-House Landing, a distance of 15 miles, sone time after midnight, where we *bivouac* for the remainder of the night.

Wednesday 8th.—Near noon, the regiment embarked on the Government transport Emily, for Washington, D. C., where they arrived after a pleasant passage, near sundown of the next day and marching to the temporary residence of our former Division General, (Brig. Gen. J. C. Robinson) who lost a leg in the late b ttles; the regiment was drawn up in line, and the officers paid their respects to the General, from thence the regiment marched to the SOLDIERS REST, where they quartered until the evening of

Friday 10th., when they took the express train, at 8 P. M., for New York, and on the morning of

Saturday 11.—About 7 A. M., arrived at Jersey City, expecting to meet there, an escort, as we had been requested, to Telegraph, on our departure from Washington, D. C.; we done as requested, but no escort arriving, we crossed the Cortlandt street Ferry, and marched to the Park Barracks, where we stacked our *arms*, and was dismissed until noon, by the req est of the Committee of the ex-members of the regiment, who had a reception in view. On the hour arriving, we drew up in 'ine, in front of the City Hall, where we was reviewed by Mayor Gunther, and marching up Broadway, without any *escort*, to Bleecker street, where we met by our old Band, (Neyer's,) and the ex-members of the regiment, who *escorted* us up the Bowery, to the Seventh regiment's Armory where we were met by a detachment from that regiment, under the command of Captain Young, who in concert with the former *escort, escorted* us to Fourteenth street, down Broadway to City Hall Park, up Broadway to the " City Guard Armory," where the regiment stacked *arms*, and partook of a COLLATION, furnished by a committee of the ex-members of the regiment, to whom all credit is due, for their kindness and courtesy, in receiving their former comrades, on the *eve* of their return to civil life. After a short time pleasantly spent, the men were dismissed, to go to their homes, with the pleasant memory, of having served their country, three years faithfully ; and thankful to a Just God, that their lives had been spared, to return home, whilst many of those who left home with them, had offered up their lives, in defence of their country, and whose names will ever be dear, to the memory of all good and loyal people. Previous to our dismissal, the City Guard Armory, was placed at our disposal, until we were mustered out of service. To Captain Young, and his men, the author in behalf of the Ninth New York State Militia, would return their sincere thanks, for his attention and kindness evinced towards them, also to the Committee, and Mr. Neyer, and his Band ; and still further to the Committee and the Militia regimen's, who had received and *escorted* the returned regiments, on their arrival in the city, for their *non-escort* and *non-réception* of as *gallant* a regiment, as there was in the United States service, during the Southern Rebellion.

From May 3d, to June 12, 1864, the regiment made fourteen marches, travelling a distance of 136 miles.

CHAPTER XIII.

Conclusion.

Monday, June 20th.—At 8 P. M., the returned members of the Ninth Regiment, New York State Militia, assembled at the St. Nicholas Hotel, pursuant to an invitation, from the ex-members of the regiment., who furnished a supper to the war-worn veterans. M. M. VanBuren, the Colonel of the regiment, before they left New York, presided at the meeting, and everything passed off pleasantly; the Supper was got up in fine stile, and with credit to the committee of Arrangements. A number of distinguished military personages were present, and all appeared to enjoy themselves; and at a seasonable hour the assemblage withdrew.

Thursday 23d.—This day, the members of the regiment, were mustered out of the United States service, where they had faithfully performed their duties to their country, for the space of three years and twenty-seven days, and returned to the pursuits of civil life.

In conclusion the author would say, that in his estimation, this regiment can show as true and as loyal a class of men, as ever laid down their lives for thecountry, and as such they will be remembered by future historians.

THE END.

RECORDS*

OF THE

NINTH REGIMENT,

NEW-YORK STATE MILITIA.

* The records of the *Ninth Regiment, New York State Militia,* were carefully compiled by the author, from official papers, and he used his utmost exertion, to have them correct; but if there should be any errors, he will willingly correct them, in future editions, upon being notified of the fact, upon their producing an honorable discharge. There are many members of this regiment who left New York, whose names will not be found recorded, consisting of those who refused to swear in at Washington, and those whose names would be a disgrace to any regiment, deserting the cause of their country, and violating the oath that they had taken to fight in its defence; the men who were DRAFTED, will not find their names recorded, although some of them, fought nobly for their country.

ORIGINAL REGIMENTAL OFFICERS,
OF THE
NINTH REGIMENT, NEW YORK STATE MILITIA.

Colonel.——John W. Stiles. resigned

Lieutenant Colonel.——William H. Halleck, died of disease

Major.——William Atterbury, promoted Lieutenant Colonel; resigned.

Surgeon.——Charles J. Nordquiest, mustered out—expiration of service

Assistant Surgeon.——Howard Pinckney, resigned

Quartermaster.——Henry L. Stevens, died of disease

Adjutant.——John B. Coppinger, resigned

Chaplain.——Rev. Benjamin T. Phillips, resigned

Sutler.——Edward Ralph, Jr.

COMPANY A.*

ORIGINAL OFFICERS

Captain.——John J. Morrison, resigned
First Lieutenant.——John Dalrymple, promoted Captain; resigned
Second Lieutenant.——Edward H. Andrews, resigned

NON-COMMISSIONED OFFICERS.

SERGEANTS.

First.——William F. Scott, discharged for disability
Second.——Eugene Pickett, promoted Captain; wounded at Antietam; resigned
Third.——Edward De Long, promoted 1st. Sergeant; discharged from wounds received at 1st. Fredericksburg
Fourth.——Edward L. Cobb, discharged for disability
Fifth.——James L. Williams, promoted 1st. Sergeant; killed at 1st. Fredericksburg

CORPORALS.

First.——Edwin Erwin, discharged for disability
Second.——William M. Winnie, discharged for disability
Third.——John Arbuckle, promoted Sergeant; discharged from wounds received at 1st Fredericksburg
Fourth.——Peter W. Johnson, promoted Sergeant-Major; wounded at Antietam; discharged by promotion
Fifth.——William C. Robinson, killed at Antietam
Sixth.——Frank F. Carter, promoted 1st. Sergeant; 2d. Lieutenant of company G.; mustered out with company G.
Seventh.——George W. Cox, discharged by promotion
Eighth.——Francis L. Lyon, discharged for disability

---

*This company left New York, with the regiment, May 27, 1861; and was mustered into the United States service, at Washington, D. C., June 8, 1861. Returned to New York, June 11, 1864; and was mustered out, June 23 1864.

PRIVATES.

A.
Amond Israel, wounded at Coal Harbor
Atkinson William, wounded at Spottsylvania

B.
Baker Edward O. promoted Corporal; discharged by promotion
Baker Edwin F. discharged for disability
Baker Thomas J. discharged for disability
Beckwith Silas, killed at 1st. Fredericksburg
Beebe Edwin, wounded at Laurel Hill; transferred to 97th N. Y. vols., June 8, 1864
Bigelow Washington, discharged for disability
Bloodgood Thomas J. mustered out with the company
Bogart Robert, wounded at Laurel Hill; transferred to 97th N. Y. vols., June 8, 1864
Brennan Christopher, wounded at Laurel Hill; transferred to 97th N. Y. vols., June 8, 1864
Buchanan David, wounded at Laurel Hill; transferred to 97th N. Y. vols., June 8, 1864
Bullman D. Lewis, discharged for disability
Byrnes Richard J. discharged for disability

C.
Chester George A. promoted Corporal; discharged by promotion
Clark James, killed in the Wilderness
Clowes Edward G. discharged by promotion
Coleman Patrick, killed at Spottsylvania
Conway Albert, discharged for disability
Crandall Orange P. wounded at Spottsylvania
Cross John, killed in the Wilderness

D.
Da Cunha John L. discharged for disability
Da Cunha Lewis, discharged for disability
De Con Francis E. discharged by promotion
Dolan Patrick, wounded in the Wilderness; transferred to 97th N. Y. vols., June 8, 1864
Duff Mathew, promoted Corporal; Sergeant; mustered out with the company
Duryea George H. discharged by order of the War Department

E.
Edgar Frederick E. transferred to the War Department; mustered out with the company
Edwards William, missing in the Wilderness, during action
Ellison Frederick, discharged from wounds received at 1st. Fredericksburg

F.

Fallon Edward A. discharged for disability
Feeks Hamlet, discharged for disability
Ferrero Emile, discharged from accidental gunshot wound
Fosdick Washington, promoted Corporal; mustered out with the company
Foster David N. promoted Corporal; wounded at 1st. Fredericksburg; promoted 2d. Lieutenant of company C.; Captain of company A.; discharged for disability
Fray Robert, killed in the Wilderness
French James C. discharged for disability

G.

Gederick Ernest, killed at Harpers Ferry
Gibson James, discharged for disability
Gillett J. Edward, discharged for disability

H.

Hance James A. killed at Antietam
Hanson John G. discharged for disability
Heath Charles H. discharged for disability
Hoaglan Isaac E. promoted 1st. Lieutenant of company B.; Captain of company H.; discharged for disability
Hodgkinson Worthington, died from wounds received at 1st. Fredericksburg
Holmwood Charles, wounded at Laurel Hill; mustered out with the company

J.

Jackson Samuel, promoted Sergeant; discharged from wounds recieved at Antietam
Johnson Daniel E. promoted Corporal; wounded at 1st. Fredericksburg
Jones Alfred, killed at 2d. Bull Run

K.

Kelley William, mustered out with the company
Kirby William H. promoted 2d. Lieutenant; discharged for disability
Kirchet Frederick, promoted Corporal; Sergeant; killed at Laurel Hill

L.

Lawrence William C. discharged from wounds received at 2d. Bull Run
Lookhirst Gottlieb, wounded in the Wilderness; transferred to 97th N. Y. vols., June 8, 1864
Luff John V. mustered out with the company

M.

Martin Andrew, discharged for disability
McCort John W. promoted Corporal; Sergeant; 2d. Lieutenant of company I; mustered out with the regiment
Mercer Alexander, killed at 2d. Bull Run
Mercer Andrew, mustered out with the company
Milden Constant, died of disease
Mitchell Joseph R. killed at 2d. Bull Run
Mitchell Thomas O. promoted Sergeant; wounded in the Wilderness; transferred to 97th N. Y. vols., June 8, 1864
Montanye Washington, discharged for disability
Moore. John D. promoted Corporal; Sergeant; 2d. Lieutenant; mustered out with the company
Murphy Edward, promoted Corporal; discharged from wounds received at Antietam

N.

Nash Samuel, discharged for disability

O.

Outwater Daniel W. promoted Corporal; 1st. Sergeant; wounded in the Wilderness; mustered out with the company

P.

Parry Henry R. discharged from wounds received at Antietam
Pearson David O. promoted Corporal; musterred out with the company
Place Warren, mustered out with the company
Porter Atwood, discharged for disability

R.

Radaman William, discharged for disability
Raymond William, discharged for disability
Roberts Samuel, discharged for disability
Roble James A. killed at 1st. Fredericksburg
Roof Smith C. discharged by promotion

S.

Sauvan Robert, discharged for disability
Scofield George H. mustered out with the company
Short James, discharged for disability
Skelly Michael W. discharged for disability
Smith Thomas, discharged for disability
Stackpole George W. discharged for disability
Stone Elias A. killed at 2d. Bull Run
Sweezy Joseph H. killed at Antietam

T.

Thompson William H. discharged for disability
Toal John T. discharged by promotion
Tufts George F. C. discharged for disability

W.

Welch William, promoted Corporal; discharged by promotion
Wheelock Edward, died from wounds received at 2d. Bull Run
Williams John L. C. discharged for disability
Woolf William, discharged for disability

Y.

Youmans William, discharged for disability

RETURNED OFFICERS.

Second Lieutenant, John D. Moore, in command of the company.

COMPANY B.*

ORIGINAL OFFICERS

Captain.——John Deppeler, resigned
First Lieutenant.——Louis Billon, resigned
Second Lieutenant.——Frederick Guyer, promoted Captain of company D.; wounded and taken prisoner in the Wilderness; exchanged and mustered out

---

NON-COMMISSIONED OFFICERS.
SERGEANTS.

First.—— Joseph A. Moesch, promoted Captain; Lieutenant Colonel; Colonel; killed in the Wilderness
Second.-——Jacob Mangold, discharged for disability
Third.——Jacob Mangold, Jr. promoted 1st. Sergeant; wounded in the Wilderness; mustered out with the company
Fourth.——John Roth, discharged for disability
Fifth.——Aug. Ginnel, promoted 1st. Sergeant; discharged by promotion

*This company left New York, with the regiment, May 27, 1861; and was mustered into the United States service, at Washington, D. C., June 8, 1861. Returned to New York, June 11, 1864; and was mustered out, June 23, 1864.

CORPORALS.

First.——Henry Perrett, promoted Sergeant; 1st. Lieutenant of company D.; Captain of company B.; wounded in the Wilderness; mustered out with the company
Second.——John Gurther, discharged for disability
Third.——Frederick Muncke, promoted Sergeant; 1st. Sergeant; 1st. Lieutenant; wounded in the Wilderness; mustered out with the company
Fourth.——George Kupper, discharged for disability
Fifth. —— Felix Hirt, promoted Sergeant; 1st. Lieutenant; killed at 1st. Fredericksburg

PRIVATES.

A.
Asal Alexander, killed at 1st. Fredericksburg

B.
Barker Charles H. promoted Corporal; Sergeant; re-enlisted; killed in the Wilderness
Bender William, discharged by promotion
Blatt John, re-enlisted; transferred to 97th N. Y. vols., June 8, 1864
Bormann Henry, died from wounds received at Antietam
Braillard Eugene, promoted Corporal; killed at 1st. Fredericksburg
Breitenstein William, wounded at 1st. Fredericksburg; ———
Briener Edward, died from wounds received at 1st. Fredericksburg
Briener Frederick, transferred to Veteran Reserve Corps
Bright Christopher, mustered out with the company
Budelmann Jacob, wounded at 1st. Fredericksburg; mustered out with the company
Buethe Frederick, wounded at 1st. Fredericksburg; transferred to Veteran Reserve Corps
Bunk Frederick, died from wounds received at Antietam

C.
Campbell Charles, discharged from wounds received at 1st. Fredericksburg
Cobb Septimes, discharged by promotion

D.
Dearman Justus, mustered out with the company;
Decan Alexander, transferred to company H. (see company H.)
Donnelly H. discharged for disability
Durand Victor, wounded at 1st. Fredericksburg; transferred to Veteran Reserve Corps

F.
Fassbind Frederick, died

G.
Gerecke Augustus, discharged from wounds received at 1st. Fredericksburg
Graff Frederick, discharged by promotion
Grant John, promoted Corporal; Sergeant; transferred to 97th N. Y. vols., June 8, 1864
Gruner Frederick, promoted Corporal; missing at 2d. Bull Run
Gyr Joseph, wounded at 1st. Fredericksburg; transferred to Veteran Reserve Corps

H.
Heinzel John, discharged from wounds received at Antietam
Hepburn John, discharged from wounds received at 1st. Fredericksburg
Huber Christopher, discharged for disability
Huber Theodore, promoted Corporal; Sergeant ; wounded in the Wilderness; mustered out with the company
Hubschle Hermann, promoted Corporal : taken prisoner. at Gettysburg, exchanged; mustered out with the company

J.
Janot George, discharged for disability
Joel Jules, mustered out with the company

K.
Kelley Patrick, died from wounds received at 1st. Fredericksburg
Keogh Thomas, promoted Corporal; Sergeant; mustered out with the company
Kriember William, wounded at 1st. Fredericksburg ; killed in the Wilderness
Krook G. discharged for disability
Kubely Augustus, promoted Corporal; wounded at Antietam; promoted Sergeant; Quartermaster Sergeant; mustered out with the company

L.
Leisinger Henry, mustered out with the company
Levy Lewis, discharged for disability
Loder J. B. discharged by order of the War Department
Lowenberg Nicholas, died from disease

M.
Mangold Henry, discharged for disability
Marchand Emile, promoted Corporal; Sergeant; wounded at 1st. Fredericksburg; promoted 2d. Lieutenant; discharged for disability

Mast Rudolph, transferred to Veteran Reserve Corps
McNider William, killed at Cedar Mountain
Moore Patrick, re-enlisted; transferred to 97th N. Y. vols., June 8, 1864
Mougnin Henry, discharged for disability
Muhlenthaler Ulrich, mustered out with the company

N.

Naumann Ernest, promoted Corporal; wounded in the Wilderness; mustered out with the company

R.

Racle G. mustered out with the company
Regener Henry, wounded at Antietam; mustered out with the company
Reinacher Emile, mustered out with the company
Reinhard John, discharged for disability
Rheinlander Henry, promoted Corporal; killed at Antietam
Rodgers Henry, died from wounds received at Antietam
Rolston James, promoted Corporal; mustered out with the company

S.

Scherrer John, taken prisoner at Gettysburg, exchanged; mustered out with the company
Schonenberg George, discharged for disability
Schrieber Gottfried, discharged for disability
Senning George, promoted Corporal; mustered out with the company
Smith George, killed at 1st. Fredericksburg
Staempfli Charles, discharged for disability
Stein Francis, transferred to Veteran Reserve Corps
Stillhammer Charles, transferred to the regular army
Sturm Charles, mustered out with the company
Switter Frederick, promoted Corporal; killed at Antietam

T.

Taylor A. H. M. discharged by order of the War Department

W.

Wiedmer Albert, re-enlisted; transferred to 97th N. Y. vols., June 8, 1864
Wisdom James, killed at 1st. Fredericksburg

Z.

Zimmermann Dominic, died from wounds received at Gettysburg

RETURNED OFFICERS.

Captain.——Henry Perrett, wounded
First Lieutenant.——Frederick Muncke, wounded

COMPANY C.*

ORIGINAL OFFICERS

Captain.——Charles E. Prescott, resigned
First Lieutenant.——Erastus R. Miller, resigned
Second Lieutenant.——William H. Draper, promoted 1st. Lieutenant; resigned

NON-COMMISSIONED OFFICERS.

SERGEANTS.

First——James H. Stevens, promoted 2d. Lieutenant; Captain; discharged for disability
Second.——Emanuel Dreyfous, promoted 1st. Sergeant; discharged for disability
Third.——Frank W. Tryon, discharged by promotion
Fourth.——Cyrus C. Hubbard, promoted 1st. Sergeant; 2d. Lieutenant; 1st. Lieutenant; Captain; mustered out with the company
Fifth.——Nathaniel T. H. Chenery, promoted 1st. Sergeant; wounded at Antietam; discharged for disability

CORPORALS.

First.——John C. Moses, discharged for disability
Second.——Charles G. Ward, promoted Sergeant; discharged by promotion
Third.——James R. Mitchell, discharged for disability
Fourth.——Edward R. Jennings, promoted Sergeant; died from disease
Fifth.——Roswell L. Van Wagenen, discharged by promotion
Sixth. ——Banker T. Morgan, discharged by promotion
Seventh.——George W. Warren, promoted Sergeant; ——
Eighth.——Fitzhugh Smith, appointed Commissary Sergeant; promoted 2d. Lieutenant of company L.; resigned

*This company left New York, with the regiment, May 27, 1861; and was mustered into the United States service, at Washington, D. C., June 8, 1861. Returned to New York, June 11, 1864; and was mustered out, June 23, 1864

PRIVATES.

A.
Anderson Charles, discharged for disability

B.
Barowsky Augustus L. promoted Corporal; transferred to 97th N. Y. vols., June 8, 1864
Bearre Charles, discharged for disability
Beckwith George W. discharged from wounds received at Antietam
Benson Edward, discharged from wounds received at Antietam
Benson John B. discharged for disability
Bierau John, killed at 1st. Fredericksburg
Bigler Henry A. discharged for disability
Bogue Willard C. wounded at Antietam; mustered out with the company
Bradley Henry C. Y. wounded at 1st. Fredericksburg; ——
Brady John B. discharged from wounds received at 1st Fredericksburg
Briggs G. P. discharged for disability
Butler Augustus P. promoted Corporal; Sergeant; 2d. Lieutenant of company A.; promoted 1st. Lieutenant of company H.; mustered out with company H.

C.
Carleton Joseph M. wounded at 1st. Fredericksburg; promoted Corporal; transferred to 97th N. Y. vols., June 8, 1864
Clackner William L. promoted Corporal; Sergeant; taken prisoner at 1st. Fredericksburg, exchanged; ——
Connolly John M. K. promoted 1st. Lieutenant of company L.; Captain of company A.; killed in the Wilderness
Crosas Andrew, discharged for disability
Cullinan Peter, promoted Corporal; wounded at 1st. Fredericksburg; promoted Sergeant; mustered out with the company

D.
Diggs Dabney W. promoted Corporal; discharged by promotion; returned to the regiment as Major; resigned
Dinkelmeyer Paul, promoted Corporal; transferred to 97th N. Y. vols., June 8, 1864
Dowers Charles W. discharged for disability
Dowers James H. discharged from wounds received at 1st. Fredericksburg

E.
Earl Henry A. promoted Corporal; ——
Egan Peter, promoted Corporal; killed at 1st. Fredericksburg

RECORDS OF COMPANY C.   11

Egbert Wesley, discharged for disability
Elmer William, discharged for disability
Engle Andrew S. Jr. promoted Corporal; taken prisoner at Gettysburg, exchanged; transferred to 97th N. Y. vols., June 8, 1864

F.

Flinn Samuel J. discharged by order
Flood Francis O. promoted Corporal; transferred to 97th N. Y. vols., June 8, 1864
Fream George L. killed by accident
Fredenburg George, discharged for disability

G.

Gray John A. transferred to gun-boat service
Green John E. promoted Corporal; discharged by promotion

H.

Hagan Mathew, transferred to 97th N. Y. vols., June 8, 1864
Hall Walter T. discharged for disability
Harmstead Robert N. discharged for disability
Hart Cornelius, discharged for disability
Hawthorne William H. promoted Corporal; wounded in the Wilderness; transferred to 97th N. Y. vols., June 8, 1864
Hays Jacob, discharged for disability
Hekking John A. discharged for disability
Hirst George O. promoted Corporal; Sergeant; wounded at 1st. Fredericksburg; promoted 1st. Sergeant; 1st. Lieutenant; mustered out with the company

I.

Iffla Abram G. discharged from wounds received at Antietam

J.

Jennings Wilton T. promoted Corporal; Sergeant; re-enlisted; transferred to 97th N. Y. vols., June 8, 1864
Johnson James E. discharged for disability
Joyce John, promoted Corporal; mustered out with the company
Joyce Samuel, discharged for disability

K.

Kennedy Daniel E. discharged for disability
King Gilbert S. promoted Corporal; Sergeant; discharged from wounds received at Antietam

L.

Lawrence George A. discharged for disability
Lynch Henry D. promoted Corporal; wounded at Gettysburg; promoted Sergeant; wounded in the Wilderness; mustered out with the company

M.

Macy Benjamin C. discharged for disability
McBride George I. taken prisoner at Gettysburg, exchanged; promoted Corporal; transferred to 97th N. Y. vols., June 8, 1864
McDonald Francis, transferred to 97th N. Y. vols., June 8, 1864
Meyer Joseph, taken prisoner at Gettysburg, exchanged; mustered out with the company
Miller John, wounded at Gettysburg ; killed in the Wilderness
Miller Louis, discharged for disability
Miller William H. promoted Corporal; discharged for wounds received at Gettysburg
Moore Lafayette, discharged for disability
Munson J. Frederick, promoted Corporal ; Sergeant ; 2d. Lieutenant ; mustered out with the company
Myers Horatio G. discharged for disability

N.

Neville John P. wounded at Antietam ; promoted Corporal ; ——
Newberry Joseph H. discharged for disability

O.

Osborne James, discharged for disability

P.

Paddock Henry T. discharged from wounds received at 1st. Fredericksburg
Parker William H. wounded at Antietam ; died of disease
Pedley William H. wounded at 1st. Fredericksburg; promoted Corporal; re-enlisted ; transferred to 97th N. Y. vols., June 8, 1864
Pierce William, discharged by order
Pryer John T discharged by promotion

Q.

Quirk Thomas W. promoted 2d. Lieutenant of company A.; wounded at 1st. Fredericksburg; promoted Captain of company A.; killed at Gettysburg

R.

Robbins William H. killed at Gettysburg
Rogers Silas W. discharged for disability
Ross Charles, discharged for disability
Russell John, discharged for disability
Russell John L. discharged for disability

S.

Schirmer Ernest, discharged by order
Sears Mathew, discharged for disability

Seybolt George H. discharged from wounds received at 1st. Fredericksburg
Sharp Isaac S. promoted Corporal; Sergeant; taken prisoner at Gettysburg, exchanged; mustered out with the company
Skinner Robert P. promoted Corporal; Sergeant, wounded at 1st Fredericksburg; promoted 1st. Sergeant; mustered out with the company
Smith Edward L. discharged for disability
Smith William Mc.C. discharged by promotion
Spackman Frederick, promoted Corporal; taken prisoner at Gettysburg, exchanged; mustered out with the company
Staples James, discharged for disability

T.

Telfair John H. promoted Corporal; mustered out with the company
Thomas Frederick, discharged for disability
Thorne Thomas W. wounded at Antietam; promoted 2d. Lieutenant; 1st. Lieutenant; and Captain of company G.; mustered out with company G.
Thorp Henry R. transferred to 97th N. Y. vols., June 8, 1864
Toland Washington S. promoted Quartermaster's Sergeant; taken prisoner on the march, exchanged; discharged by order
Travis Robert P. transferred to 97th N. Y. vols., June 8, 1864
Tyson Clarence F. killed at 1st. Fredericksburg

U.

Uhl Charles, promoted Corporal; discharged for disability

V.

Van Camp John, discharged from wounds received at 1st. Fredericksburg
Van Duersen John, discharged from wounds received at Antietam
Van Pelt Gilbert S. discharged for disability

W.

Warner Frederick R. wounded at Harpers Ferry; promoted Corporal; discharged for disability
Watson Frederick A. discharged by promotion
White George H. discharged for disability
White John F. Jr. taken prisoner at Gettysburg, exchanged; promoted Corporal; transferred to 97th N. Y. vols., June 8, 1864
Whitman J. A. discharged for disability
Woodhull A. E. discharged by promotion
Woodruff H. C. discharged for disability

DRUMMER.

Fleming Edward, discharged for disability

RETURNED OFFICERS.

Captain.—— Cyrus C. Hubbard
First Lieutenant.——George O. Hirst
Second Lieutenant.-——J. Frederick Munson

COMPANY D.*

ORIGINAL OFFICERS

Captain.——John W. Davis, resigned
First Lieutenant. ——Edward R. Greene, promoted Captain; resigned
Second Lieutenant.——James B. Van Beuren, promoted 1st. Lieutenant; resigned

NON-COMMISSIONED OFFICERS.

SERGEANTS.

First.——William S. Striker, promoted 2d. Lieutenant; transferred to Signal Corps
Second.——Ralph A. Lanning, promoted 1st. Lieutenant; Captain; wounded at Antietam; resigned
Third.——Henry P. Clare, promoted 1st. Sergeant; 1st. Lieutenant; appointed Adjutant; mustered out with th regiment
Fourth.——Isaac Seymour, jr., discharged by promotion
Fifth.——Louis A. Kohly, discharged by promotion

CORPORALS.

First.——William A. Rice, promoted 1st. Sergeant; discharged for disability
Second.-——Henry Osgood, promoted 1st. Sergeant; died from wounds received at 1st. Fredericksburg
Third.——James A. Johnson, discharged by promotion
Fourth.——Frank G. Aims, promoted Sergeant; died of disease

*This company left New York, with the regiment, May 27, 1861; and was mustered into the United States service, at Washington, D. C., June 8, 1861. Returned to New York, June 11, 1864; and was mustered out, June 23, 1864.

Fifth.——Julien F. Allen, promoted 2d. Lieutenant of company I.
Sixth.——Leonard W. Denham, promoted Sergeant; discharged by promotion
Seventh.——Charles B. Lamb, promoted Sergeant; discharged for disability
Eighth.——Daniel W. Lee, discharged by promotion

PRIVATES.

A.

Amory James, detached
Askwith James, died from wounds received at 1st. Fredericksburg

B.

Bayerle Bernard, promoted Sergeant ; discharged for disability
Beers Jacob H. promoted Commissary Sergeant; discharged for disability
Beers Joseph F. discharged for disability
Benson Demilt S. discharged for disability
Briggs Henry W. discharged for disability
Brinkerhoff James F. discharged for disability
Burnham George E. promoted Sergeant; transferred to 97th N. Y. vols., June 8, 1864
Butler John, died from wounds received at 1st. Fredericksburg
Butler William F. killed at 2d. Bull Run

C.

Carson William, discharged for disability
Cashman William, transferred to Signal Corps
Chave William, promoted Sergeant; discharged for disability
Clark William, discharged for disability
Coleman George B. wounded at 1st. Fredericksburg; discharged by promotion
Corbin Thomas F. promoted Corporal; mustered out with the company

D.

Dean Herman B. discharged for disability
Dolan John B. promoted 2d. Lieutenant of company B. ; 1st. Lieutenant of company A. mustered out with company A.
Dominick Charles C. transferred to 97th N. Y. vols., June 8, 1864
Durbrow Washington, wounded at 1st. Fredericksburg; discharged by promotion
Durnin Eugene, discharged by promotion

F.

Fisher Edward F. discharged by promotion

G

Gardiner Horace H. discharged by promotion
Gardiner Lewis J. discharged by promotion
Garrison Robert D. killed at 2d. Bull Run
Geib Adam, promoted Corporal; mustered out with the company
Gesner Charles H. discharged by promotion
Gilbert William H. promoted Corporal; transferred to 97th N. Y. vols., June 8, 1864
Graves John B. promoted Corporal; discharged for wounds received at 1st. Fredericksburg
Gray William, transferred to the regular army

H.

Hibbard William H. transferred to 97th N. Y. vols., June 8, 1864
Holdredge Joseph S. discharged for disability
Hull Charles H. wounded at Antietam; detailed in Washington; mustered out with the company
Hyatt George E. detailed in the Ambulance Corps; transferred to 97th N. Y. vols., June 8, 1864

I.

Isaacs Montefeiro M. discharged by promotion

J.

Jaques John W. transferred to gun-boat service, taken sick, and returned to company; wounded at Antietam; 1st. Fredericksburg; and in the Wilderness; transferred to 97th N. Y. vols., June 8, 1864
Jones Fennimore P. discharged for disability

K.

Kemmerer Isaac B. wounded at Antietam; detailed in Washington; mustered out with the company
Kennia John R. discharged for disability
King William H. discharged for disability

L.

Lambert Francis, died from wounds received at Antietam
Laycraft Thomas J. discharged for disability
Leslie Alexander, wounded Antietam; discharged from wounds received at 1st. Fredericksburg
Lewis J. Woodruff, discharged by promotion
Lohn George, discharged from wounds received at Antietam
Lyon Edward H. discharged for disability

M.

Mallory William, discharged for disability
Martin James, discharged from wounds received at Antietam
Martin James J. discharged for disability

Maurice Samuel, discharged for disability
McCance William, promoted Corporal; 1st. Sergeant; wounded at Gettysburg; mustered out with the company
McKie William, mustered out with the company
McNally Samuel, discharged by promotion
Miles Alfred, discharged for disability
Mollesson Theophilus M. discharged by promotion
Montgomery Alexander, detailed at the Division Head Quarters; mustered out with the company
Mosher Theodore, transferred to 97th N. Y. vols., June 8, 1864
Mykens Thomas W. killed at Antietam

N.
Nice William, transferred to Signal Corps

O.
Ohl William H. discharged for disability

P.
Phelps James H. transferred to 97th N. Y. vols., June 8, 1864
Phelps John S. killed at Antietam
Pollock Joseph B. discharged for disability
Pollock Thomas C. accidental death
Price Edward A. discharged from wounds received at Antietam

R.
Ring Franklin M. discharged by promotion
Richie Jacob; discharged from wounds received at Antietam
Roberts Philip R. discharged by promotion
Rodgers Leonard, died of disease
Ryder William S. detailed in Washington, D. C.; re-enlisted; transferred to 97th N. Y. vols., June 8, 1864

S.
Salter William, promoted Corporal; discharged for disability
Schermerhorn Horace, discharged from wounds received at Antietam
Selheimer David C. discharged by promotion
Seymour Fitz James, discharged for disability
Sheridan James, wounded and missing at 2d. Bull Run
Simonson Cornelius A. discharged by promotion
Sinclair Charles D. promoted Sergeant; transferred to 97th N. Y. vols., June 8, 1864
Sinclair James, discharged for disability
Springer John W. re-enlisted in company L.; transferred to 97th N. Y. vols., June 8, 1864
Stiles Andrew B, promoted 2d. Lieutenant of company L.: resigned

Street Henry, wounded at Antietam; missing during action, at 1st. Fredericksburg

T.

Taylor Asa W. discharged from wounds received at Antietam
Taylor John G. tranferred to regular army
Therriott Alfred, discharged for disability

V.

Van Beuren Charles T. discharged for disability
Van Beuren William H. died from wounds received at Antietam
Van Sicklan Samuel, discharged from wounds received at 1st. Fredericksburg
Van Walkenburgh Tremain W. wounded at 1st. Fredericksburg ; Mustered out with the company
Vredenburgh John, discharged for disability
Vredenburgh Sidney J. promoted Corporal; transferred to 97th N. Y. vols., June 8, 1864

W.

Wall Theodore M. discharged from wounds received at 1st. Fredericksburg
Watson George, Jr. promoted Sergeant ; discharged by promotion
Weaver Theodore, missing at 2d. Bull Run
Wheelock Erastus, discharged for disability
White Carter S. discharged for disability
White Robert, discharged from wounds received at 1st. Fredericksburg
Wight Frederick H. wounded at Antietam ; detailed in Washington ; transferred to 97th N. Y. vols., June 8, 1864
Wilson Charles H. wounded in the Wilderness ; mustered out with the company
Wing Lucius C. promoted Sergeant; wounded at Spottsylvania; mustered out with the company

Y.

Yates Samuel L discharged for disability

RETURNED OFFICERS.

Captain.——Frederick Guyer, wounded and taken prisoner
First Lieutenant. — Frank Paige, formerly of company G.
Second Lieutenant.——Charles W. Reynolds, killed

COMPANY E.*

ORIGINAL OFFICERS

Captain.——Henry C. Smith, resigned
First Lieutenant.——Henry C. Brooks, resigned
Second Lieutenant.——William T. Galbraith, resigned

NON-COMMISSIONED OFFICERS.

SERGEANTS.

First.——Edwin R. Reed, discharged by promotion
Second. —— Stephen Marvin, discharged for disability
Fifth.——Frank C. Alger, promoted 1st. Sergeant; 1st. Lieutenant; resigned

CORPORALS.

First.——William Ferguson, discharged for disability
Second.——Alonzo Craw, died of disease

PRIVATES.

B.

Beauche August O. killed at 2d. Bull Run
Beers Henry W. discharged for disability
Bladen Charles, mustered out with the company
Blakelock Richard J. discharged by order
Briggs George S. discharged for disability
Brooks George W. mustered out with the company
Brown Archibald, discharged from wounds received at Antietam
Burt Charles A. discharged by promotion

---

*This company left New York, with the regiment, May 27, 1861; and was mustered into the United States service, at Washington, D. C., June 8, 1861. Returned to New York, June 11, 1864; and was mustered out, June 23, 1864.

C.

Campbell Archibald, transferred to 97th N. Y. vols., June 8, 1864
Carlisle John, discharged for disability
Chadeayne Henry A. wounded at Antietam; discharged by promotion
Coffin Frank W. detailed at Division Head-Quarters; mustered out with the company
Collins John J. transferred to 97th N. Y. vols., June 8, 1864
Concklin Nathaniel A. discharged by promotion
Connery John J. promoted Corporal; Sergeant; discharged from wounds received at 1st. Fredericksburg
Cook Moses F. transferred to 97th N. Y. vols., June 8, 1864
Cook Robert F. promoted Corporal; 1st. Sergeant; wounded at 1st. Fredericksburg; promoted 2d. Lieutenant of company F.; mustered out with company F.
Cook William H. discharged for disability

D.

Davis Thomas J. promoted Corporal; mustered out with the company
Devins John J. discharged for disability
Dixon Thomas, discharged for disability
Donahue John, discharged for disability

E.

Esterly Peter A. wounded at 2d. Bull Run; wounded in the Wilderness; mustered out with the company

F.

Falon Augustus, killed at 1st. Fredericksburg
Fargo Elanson J. wounded at 1st. Fredericksburg; transferred to 97th N. Y. vols., June 8, 1864
Floyd Samuel, discharged for disability
Frederick William, discharged from wounds received at Antietam
Freeman Mathew, died of disease

G.

Gillan David, mustered out with the company
Gould William F. mustered out with the company

H.

Hale Frederick E. discharged for disability
Hale William E. discharged from wounds received at Antietam
Hemma Thomas, transferred to Veteran Reserve Corps
Henderson William E. promoted Sergeant; died from wounds received in the Wilderness
Heffren George, transferred to 97th N. Y. vols., June 8, 1864
Hennion Thomas M. mustered out with the company

Hinton Henry L. transferred to Veteran Reserve Corps
Hodges George H. discharged for disability
Holmes Joseph H. discharged for disability
Hopper John J. discharged for disability
Hopper Joseph C. discharged from wounds received at Antietam
Houseman Nicholas V. discharged for disability
How Storer W. discharged by promotion
Howell Isaac, died of disease

J.

Jefferds Edward J. discharged for disability
Jordan Albert F. transferred to 97th. N. Y. vols., June 8, 1864
Jordan Frank E. promoted 2d. Lieutenant; mustered out with the
    company

K.

King Edward, discharged for disability

L.

Layton Thomas, promoted Corporal; 2d. Lieutenant; killed at
    1st. Fredericksburg
Le Roy Alphonse, mustered out with the company
Lewis Albert, killed at 1st. Fredericksburg
Lymbeck John, promoted Sergeant; discharged for disability
Lynch Peter A. discharged from wounds received at 2d. Bull Run
Lyons Charles F. discharged for disability

M.

Malone John, died from wounds received at 1st, Fredericksburg
McCreary Archibald, discharged from wounds received at 1st.
    Fredericksburg
McDade Charles, promoted Corporal; Sergeant; mustered out
    with the company
McKenzie Gerard L. discharged by promotion
McKenzie J. H. discharged for disability
Moore Thomas, kileed in the Wilderness
Morgan David A. killed at 1st. Fredericksburg
Morgan William, discharged for disability

N.

Nevius Edward W. discharged for disability
Nodine William H. discharged for disability
Northrup Phillip, discharged for disability

P.

Parkinson William F. died of disease
Patterson Samuel, discharged for disability
Payne Charles, discharged for disability
Peal George W. transferred to regular army

22   RECORDS OF COMPANY E.

Penrose Edward B. wounded at Antietam; mustered out with the company
Peters Clarence, discharged for disability

R.

Rawley Thomas, discharged for disability
Ready Charles, discharged for disability
Riley John, discharged from wounds received at Antietam
Royce Edward J. discharged from wounds received at Antietam

S.

Salter George W. discharged by order
Sands David, transferred to gun-boat service
Savard Charles, mustered out with company
Scott James A. discharged for disability
Scott Samuel, wounded in the Wilderness; transferred to 97th N. Y. vols., June 8, 1864
Shanley Edward, promoted 1st. Lieutenant; Captain; resigned
Simmonds Lemuel, discharged for disability
Simpson William, discharged by promotion
Sitter J. W. discharged for disability
Smith George F. discharged for disability
Smith Henry H. discharged for disability
Smith William H. discharged from wounds received in the Wilderness
Sprague James E. promoted Corporal; Sergeant; mustered out with the company
Stamburn James W. discharged by order
Stewart Archibald, transferred to 97th N. Y. vols., June 8, 1864
Stewart George W. transferred to the Navy
Sykes Benjamin C. discharged for disability

T.

Taylor E. J. discharged for disability
Teller Lawrence, transferred to 97th N. Y. vols., June 8, 1864
Terry Addison F. discharged from wounds received at 1st. Fredericksburg
Terwilliger Josiah C. promoted Corporal; Sergeant; mustered out with the company
Trrittenbach J. J. discharged for disability

V.

Van Schaick Dunnell, transferred to Signal Corps
Voorhis Daniel, discharged for disability

W.

Wagner Rufus, died of disease
Wilkins Charles F. discharged for disability

Wilkinson Albert, discharged from wounds received at 2d. Bull
    Run
Williams John, transferred to 97th N. Y. vols., June 8, 1864
Wright George A. discharged for disability

Y.

Yeomans J. died of disease

DRUMMER.

Springer Hezekiah, transferred to Veteran Reserve Corps

RETURNED OFFICERS.

Captain.——Lawrence Whitney, formerly of company F.
First Lieutenant.——Thomas Howard, formerly of company F.
Second Lieutenant.——Frank Jordan

COMPANY F.*

ORIGINAL OFFICERS

Captain.—— Allan Rutherford, promoted Major; Lieutenant Colonel; resigned

First Lieutenant.——Charles R. Braine, transferred to Signal Corps

Second Lieutenant.—— Angus Cameron, promoted Captain; wounded at 1st. Fredericksburg; resigned

Brevet Second Lieutenant.——Robert G. Rutherford, promoted 1st. Lieutenant; Captain of company G.; resigned

NON-COMMISSIONED OFFICERS.

SERGEANTS.

First.——Frederick C. Alden, discharged for disability
Second.——Henry Cushing, discharged by promotion
Third.——Charles S. Strong, promoted 1st. Sergeant; 2d. Lieutenant; appointed Adjutant; resigned
Fourth.——Edward W. Greene, discharged for disability
Fifth.——John H. Hennell, promoted 1st. Sergeant; discharged by promotion

CORPORALS.

First.——William L. Siners, discharged for disability
Second.——Ira W. Stewart, discharged by promotion
Third.——James Davison, discharged for disability
Fourth.——Stephen W. Crandell, mustered out with the company
Fifth.——Roland H. Withers, discharged by promotion
Sixth.——Jacob Jacobs, promoted Sergeant; 1st. Lieutenant; Captain; wounded at Gettysburg; mustered out with the company

---

*This company left New York, with the regiment, May 27, 1861; and was mustered into the United States service, at Washington, D. C., June 8, 1861. Returned to New York, June 11, 1864; and was mustered out, June 23, 1864.

Seventh.——Daniel Trittenbach, promoted Sergeant; mustered out with the company
Eighth.——Henry Buermeyer, promoted Sergeant; 1st. Lieutenant; wounded in the Wilderness; mustered out with the company

PRIVATES.

A.

Acker Abijah F. promoted Corporal; mustered out with the company
Ackerman Abram, discharged for disability
Alphonse Edward C. promoted Sergeant; discharged for disability
Archer Charles, promoted Corporal; Sergeant; mustered out with the company
Armstrong Theodore, transferred to the 97th N. Y. vols., June 8, 1864
Atwell William C. discharged for disability

B.

Barnes Edward L. discharged by promotion
Barnes Thomas S. discharged for disability
Barnes William J. promoted 2d. Lieutenant; taken prisoner, at Gettysburg, and not exchanged, till long after his company had been mustered out
Benner John, promoted Corporal; Sergeant; killed at 1st. Fredericksburg
Berry Samuel, wounded at Antietam; promoted Corporal; wounded in the Wilderness; transferred to 97th N. Y. vols., June 8, 1864
Bissell Eugene, discharged for disability
Blakeney Jacob M. discharged for disability
Blakeney Joseph H. killed at 2d. Bull Run
Broach George H. discharged for disability
Broach James H. discharged for disability
Brown Isaac, discharged for disability
Burtis James, promoted Corporal; Sergeant; wounded at Gettysburg; promoted 1st. Sergeant; mustered out with the company

C.

Cassady Thomas, promoted Corporal; taken prisoner at Gettysburg, exchanged; mustered out with the company
Clough Edward H. discharged from wounds received at Antietam

Coe Henry O. discharged for disability
Coe Luther R. promoted Corporal ; discharged for disability
Cossman William H. promoted Corporal; died from wounds received at Antietam
Cram Henry O. discharged for disability
Cunningham Richard, discharged for disability

D.

Davis Joseph B. promoted Sergeant ; re-enlisted; transferred to 97th N. Y. vols., June 8, 1864
Doherty James H. discharged for disability
Du Bell John, discharged for disability

F.

Fister George, transferred to 97th N. Y. vols., June 8, 1864
Flynn Thomas, discharged for disability
Frazee Samuel C. promoted Corporal ; wounded at Gettysburg; promoted Sergeant; mustered out with the company

G.

Goodwin Charles, jr. discharged by promotion
Goodwin William, discharged for disability
Greene Thomas B. discharged by promotion
Graves Orlow H. transferred to the regular army

H.

Haggerty John, discharged for disability
Halliday James R. discharged for disability
Hand Silas H. discharged for disability
Hanna Thomas L. wounded at Antietam; promoted Corporal ; transferred by order
Hatfield Alfred R. discharged for disability
Haviland Thomas G. discharged for disability
Hermance William L. discharged by promotion
Hinchman James, died of disease
Howard Thomas, promoted Corporal ; Sergeant; 1st. Lieutenant; mustered out with the company
Hunt Hiram L. wounded at Antietam; transferred to Veteran Reserve Corps
Huntington Isaac L. promoted 1st. Lieutenant; wounded at 2d. Bull Run; resigned
Hyatt Joshua F. mustered out with the company

J.

Johnson Alfred R. discharged for disability

K.

Kelley Benjamin F. discharged for disability
Kemble Thomas W. discharged from wounds received at Antietam

L.
Lathrop Clarence H. discharged for disability
Lincoln Charles R. discharged for disability
Lippett Ceylon O. transferred to Veteran Reserve Corps
Lounsberry Stephen, discharged for disability
Luffberry George, discharged for disability

M.
Maxwell George, transferred to 97th N. Y. vols., June 8, 1864
McKenzie George, discharged by order
McNally Frank, discharged for disability
Millspaugh James L. discharged by promotion
Munson Reuben S. promoted Corporal; Sergeant; discharged for disability

N.
Nesbitt Charles, mustered out with the company

O.
Osborne William B. taken prisoner at 2d. Bull Run, exchanged; promoted Corporal; mustered out with the company

P.
Palmer Carlton, discharged by promotion
Pancoast George W. discharged from wounds received at Antietam
Penney Alfred R. transferred to 97th N. Y. vols., June 8, 1864
Penny Archibald, promoted Corporal; Sergeant; killed in the Wilderness
Pinkham William E. wounded at 1st. Fredricksburg; transferred to Veteran Reserve Corps
Prince William, wounded at Antietam; discharged by promotion

R.
Reaney John, transferred to 97th N. Y. vols., June 8, 1864
Reynolds Charles F. promoted 2d. Lieutenant of company D.; killed in the Wilderness
Russell Charles F. wounded at 1st. Fredericksburg; mustered out with the company
Ryding William L. discharged for disability

S.
Scaich Joseph, jr. discharged by promotion
Scott William, wounded at 1st. Fredericksburg; promoted Corporal; mustered out with the company
Shephard Mathew H. discharged from wounds received at 1st. Fredericksburg
Simmons Daniel, jr. wounded at 1st. Fredericksburg; transferred to Veteran Reserve Corps

Simmons John S. mustered out with the company
Soderberry Robert A. promoted Corporal; commissary Sergeant; mustered out with the company
Spaulding Charles F. promoted Corporal; Sergeant; discharged from wounds received at 1st. Fredericksburg
Steves Jacob W. mustered out with the company
Storer Abner R. promoted Corporal; Sergeant; discharged for disability
Sullivan Cornelius, discharged for disability

T.

Thompson George H. promoted Corporal; mustered out with the company

V.

Van Name William B. discharged by promotion
Van Whyck John, discharged by promotion
Van Zandt Washington, discharged for disability
Vaulk Lawrence B. discharged for disability

W.

Washburne William R. discharged for disability
Weeks Caleb D. discharged by promotion
Weeks Noah L. discharged by promotion
White Orion, discharged from wounds received at Antietam
Whitney Lawrence M. promoted 1st. Lieutenant of company E.; wounded at Gettysburg; promoted Captain of company E.; mustered out with company E.
Williams John H. promoted Corporal; wounded at Antietam; discharged for disability
Wilson William, transferred to the 97th N. Y. vols., June 8, 1864

DRUMMERS.

Rockett John, mustered out with the company
Bohnenberger George, mustered out with the company

RETURNED OFFICERS.

Captain.——Jacob Jacobs
First Lieutenant. ——Thomas Howard
Second Lieutenant.——Henry Buermeyer, wounded

COMPANY G.*

ORIGINAL OFFICERS

Captain.——William H. Atterbury, promoted Major; Lieutenant Colonel; resigned
First Lieutenant.——John Hendrickson, promoted Captain; Major; Lieutenant Colonel; wounded at 1st. Fredericksburg; promoted Colonel; resigned
Second Lieutenant.——Joseph D. Wickham, resigned
Brevet Second Lieutenant.——David W. Anderson, promoted 2d. Lieutenant; resigned

NON-COMMISSIONED OFFICERS.
SERGEANTS.

First.——Matthew S. Gregory, promoted 1st Lieutenant; resigned
Second.——William F. Terwilliger, promoted 1st. Lieutenant; wounded at Antietam; resigned
Third.——Theodore W. Vandegriff, discharged from wounds received at Antietam;
Fourth.——Frank Paige, wounded at 1st. Fredericksburg; promoted 1st. Lieutenant of company D.; mustered out with company D.
Fifth.——Charles A. Clark, wounded at Antietam; promoted 1st. Lieutenant of company B.; killed at Gettysburg

CORPORALS.

First.——Charles W. Beecher, killed at Antietam
Second.——Samuel S. J. Briggs, promoted 1st. Sergeant of company L.; discharged by promotion
Third.——Joel R. Woodruff, discharged by promotion
Fifth.——James P. Spencer, discharged for disability
Sixth.——Marcus Miller, discharged for disability
Seventh.——Dudley Murray, discharged for disability
Eighth.——Sayers Hadley, transferred to the Veteran Reserve Corps

*This company left New York, with the regiment, May 27, 1861; and was mustered into the United States service, at Washington, D. C., June 8, 1861. Returned to New York, June 11, 1864; and was mustered out, June 23, 1864.

PRIVATES.

A.
Allen Edward G. mustered out with the company

B.
Banks John E. killed at Harpers Ferry
Bolander Charles J. mustered out with the company
Bradley Bradford D. discharged for disability
Bramhill William E. transferred to regular army
Brevoort Henry, discharged by promotion
Brown James, transferred to Artillery
Burge Sydney A. transferred to Veteran Reserve Corps
Buxton George J. discharged for disability

C.
Carpenter James H. discharged for disability
Center John, jr. discharged for disability
Clifford Thomas D. promoted 1st. Sergeant; taken prisoner in the Wilderness; transferred to 97th N. Y. vols., June 8, 1864
Conlin John, transferred to Veteran Reserve Corps

D.
Dalton Michael, discharged from wounds received at Antietam
Dennison H. Bedell, discharged by promotion
Donaldson Sovereign A. transferred to 97th N. Y. vols., June 8, 1864
Downing John A. discharged for disability
Ducy John E. mustered out with the company
Durand James, jr. discharged from wounds received at Antietam

F.
Faitoute James B. discharged for disability
Farley James B. wounded at 2d. Bull Run;
Fleming Dennis, wounded at Gettysburg; promoted Corporal; mustered out with the company
Foy William, killed at Antietam

G.
Gardner Augustus, taken prisoner at Gettysburg, exchanged; mustered out with the company
Garthwaite Andrew J. discharged from wounds received at 2d. Bull Run
Graley Joseph O. discharged by promotion
Grogan Thomas R. killed at Antietam
Guest Benjamin, wounded at Antietam; mustered out with the company

H.

Hegeman James H. discharged for disability
Holden James M. discharged for disability
Howell George H. transferred to Artillery
Hoyt James H. discharged by promotion
Hoyt John H. died of disease
Hurd Charles W. B. killed at Antietam

J.

Jessup Hiram W. transferred to regular army
Jones Isaac P. taken prisoner at Gettysburg, exchanged; mustered out with the company

K.

Keenan Thomas, promoted Sergeant; wounded in the Wilderness; transferred to 97th N. Y. vols., June 8, 1864
Kelley Bartley, discharged from wounds received at Antietam
Kelley William H. discharged for disability
Kiley Thomas, killed at 2d. Bull Run
Knapp William A. discharged by promotion

L.

Lacoste James, discharged for disability
Lamberton Henry B. discharged for disability
Lawson William H. wounded at 1st. Fredericksburg; mustered out with the company
Le Barnes Edward A. killed at 2d. Bull Run

M.

Macauley Charles, mustered out with the company
Martin Robert, taken prisoner at Gettysburg, exchanged; wounded in the Wilderness; transferred to 97th N. Y. vols., June 8, 1864
May William, transferred to Artillery
McLaughlin Charles A. transferred to regular army
McMahon Andrew, discharged from wounds received at Antietam
Mitchell Mathew C. discharged for disability
Morris William S. promoted 1st. Lieutenant; wounded in the Wilderness; mustered out with the company
Morrissey James, discharged from wounds received at Antietam
Munday F. Henry, discharged from wounds received at 1st. Fredericksburg
Murray Cyrus C. discharged for disability

N.

Noman John A. discharged by promotion

P.

Parks James, transferred to regular army
Parton John R. wounded at Antietam; promoted Corporal; mustered out with the company
Pitts John, mustered out with the company
Polster Arnold, promoted Sergeant; mustered out with the company
Power Edward, wounded at 1st. Fredericksburg; transferred to Veteran Reserve Corps
Purcell Michael, wounded at Antietam; promoted Sergeant; taken prisoner in the Wilderness, and not exchanged, till long after his company had been mustered out

R.

Reuss George P. killed at 1st. Fredericksburg
Rhodes William W. discharged from wounds received at Antietam
Robbins Archibald J. discharged for disability

S.

Senical Joseph P. discharged for disability
Shafford George E. promoted Sergeant; wounded and taken prisoner in the Wilderness, exchanged; transferred to 97th N. Y. vols., June 8, 1864
Sharot Joseph, wounded at 2d. Bull Run; mustered out with the company
Sheffield Benjamin J. died of disease
Sleight Samuel F. discharged from wounds received at 2d. Bull Run
Smith John C. transferred to Veteran Reserve Corps
Sniffon James B. discharged for disability
Stewart Charles H. re-enlisted; transferred to 97th N. Y. vols., June 8, 1864
Stroub Frederick A. discharged for disability
Swenarton Thomas H. discharged for disability

T.

Teale George W. promoted Hospital Steward; mustered out with the company
Thompson Richard, discharged for disability
Tomlins John E. died of disease
Topping George W. promoted Coproral; killed at Laurel Hill

V.

Valentine Frederick F. discharged for disability
Voorhies Joseph H. discharged from wounds eceived at Antietam

W.

Washburn George W. wounded at Fredericksburg; mustered out with the company

Watkeys Edward H. discharged for disability
Watson Robert H. discharged from wounds received at Antietam
Weaver James G. wounded at 1st. Fredericksburg; promoted Corporal; wounded in the Wilderness; transferred to 97th N. Y. vols., June 8, 1864
White Alasco C. promoted Sergeant; discharged from wounds received at Antietam
Williamson Henry V. wounded at Harpers Ferry; promoted Sergeant of company L.; 2d. Lieutenant; 1st. Lieutenant; Captain; Major; mustered out with the regiment
Wood Daniel; re-enlisted; wounded in the Wilderness; transferred to 97th N. Y. vols., June 8, 1864
Wood Lyman, discharged for disability

Y.

Yerance Peter, transferred to 97th N. Y. vols., June 8, 1864

DRUMMER.

Swords Joseph F. mustered out with the company

RETURNED OFFICERS.

Captain.——Thomas W. Thorne, formerly of company C.
First Lieutenant.——William S. Morris, wounded
Second Lieutenant.——Frank F. Carter, formerly of company A. wounded

COMPANY H.*

ORIGINAL OFFICERS

Captain.——George Tuthill, resigned
First Lieutenant.——John T. Lockman, promoted Captain, resigned
Second Lieutenant.——Charles E. Tuthill, promoted Adjutant; resigned

* This company left New York, with the regiment, May 27, 1861; and was mustered into the United States service, at Washington, D. C., June 8, 1861. Returned to New York, June 11, 1864; and was mustered out, June 23, 1864.

NON-COMMISSIONED OFFICERS.

SERGEANTS.

First.——John Clements, promoted 2d. Lieutenant; resigned
Second.——John H. Reid, mustered out with the company
Third. ——John Ponsonby, discharged for disability
Fourth.——Isaac Lockman, promoted 1st. Lieutenant; resigned
Fifth.——De Witt C. Hammond, promoted 2d. Lieutenant; re signed

CORPORALS.

First.——Richard Fosdick, promoted 1st. Sergeant; discharged for disability
Second.——James Denin, promoted Sergeant; 2d. Lieutenant; resigned
Third.——William H. Ponsonby, discharged for disability
Fourth.——Richard Van Riper, discharged for disability
Fifth.——Henry A. Van Pelt, promoted Corporal; Sergeant; 1st. Lieutenant; Captain; resigned
Sixth.——William Gibson, discharged for disability
Seventh.-——William H. Roberts, promoted to 2d. Lieutenant; resigned
Eighth.——Warren Chapman, promoted Sergeant; discharged for disability

PRIVATES.

A.

Adee Joseph W. jr. re-enlisted; transferred to 97th N. Y. vols., June 8, 1864
Albro Joshua C. discharged for disability
Allard Edmund B. transferred to Veteran Reserve Corps

B.

Baker John L. promoted Corporal; mustered out with the company
Barnes Thomas C. transferred to 97th N. Y. vols., June 8, 1864
Beggs Joseph, mustered out with the company
Bell David, discharged for disability
Belton Thomas H. mustered out with the company
Brewer George, discharged by promotion
Bresnaw Jerry, died of wounds received at Antietam
Brockner Edwin O. promoted Corporal; transferred to 97th N. Y. vols., June 8, 1864

Brockner William, transferred to Veteran Reserve Corps
Bruun Henry, missing in action at 2d. Bull Run
Burns Patrick, killed at Gettysburg
Buskirk Theodore, discharged for disability

C.

Caffrey John, died of disease
Christie John, discharged by order
Clearman John, discharged by order
Coburn Robert S. transferred to 97th N. Y. vols., June 8, 1864
Coffey John J. mustered out with the company
Conley George A. promoted Corporal; mustered out with the company

D.

Daly John, missing in action at Thoroughfare Gap
Daly William, appointed drummer; transferred to 97th N. Y. vols., June 8, 1864
Davis Edmund A. mustered out with the company
Deacon Thomas, mustered out with the company
De Con Alexander, killed at Antietam
Devlin David, promoted Corporal; Sergeant; wounded at Spottsylvania; transferred to 97th N. Y. vols., June 8, 1864
Devlin Joseph, promoted Corporal; wounded in the Wilderness; mustered out with the company
Dowling Joseph, transferred to 97th N. Y. vols., June 8, 1864
Drew George, mustered out with the company
Dupignac Richard, discharged for disability

F.

Flaack Lewis, discharged for disability

G.

Gidley Lewis, mustered out with the company
Gulick John L. discharged for disability

H.

Hallenbeck John N. discharged for disability
Hallock Joseph T. promoted Corporal; Sergeant; wounded in the Wilderness; mustered out with the company
Hathaway Stephen, discharged for disability
Harriott George A. wounded at 1st. Fredericksburg; mustered out with the company
Hart Jacob, transferred to 97th N. Y. vols., June 8, 1864
Heenan James, died of disease
Holmes Isaac, wounded at 1st. Fredericksburg; mustered out with the company

K.

Kane John J. promoted Corporal; discharged for disability
Kearney Charles, mustered out with the company
Killman William F. promoted Corporal; Sergeant; mustered out with the company
Kirby William S. promoted Sergeant; wounded at Antietam; transferred to Veteran Reserve Corps
Knight Thomas, transferred to 97th N. Y. vols., June 8, 1864

L.

Larkin John, wounded at 1st. Fredericksburg; promoted Corporal; Sergeant; wounded in the Wilderness; transferred to 97th N. Y. vols., June 8, 1864

M.

Mahnken John, wounded at 1st. Fredericksburg; transferred to Veteran Reserve Corps
Martin Frank, discharged from wounds received at Antietam
Maze Augustus B. discharged by order
Miller William, died of disease
Millinett William F. promoted Corporal; mustered out with the company
McCourt Henry, wounded at 1st. Fredericksburg; transferred to Veteran Reserve Corps
McDermott John, mustered out with the company
McDermott Thomas, discharged for disability
McGrath Joseph, re-enlisted; transferred to 97th N. Y. vols., June 8, 1864
McLane James, mustered out with the company
Murphy Matthew, killed at Antietam

O.

O'Brien William, discharged for disability
O'Connor Henry, discharged by order
O'Connor James, discharged by promotion
O'Connor James A. wounded in the Wilderness; transferred to 97th N. Y. vols., June 8, 1864
O'Neill Charles, taken prisoner at 2d. Bull Run, exchanged; re-enlisted; transferred to 97th N. Y. vols., June 8, 1864

P.

Pelton Henry F. mustered out with the company
Pinard Nelson, transferred to gun-boat service
Poillon Clark C. discharged for disability
Peirson Ira A. discharged for disability

R.

Russell William H. transferred to Veteran Reserve Corps
Ryan Thomas J. transferred to 97th N. Y. vols., June 8, 1864

S.

Shrimpton William H. missing in action at 2d. Bull Run
Skeats Charles, promoted Corporal; mustered out with the company
Smith John H. promoted Sergeant; mustered out with the company
Smith George E. wounded at 1st. Fredericksburg; promoted Corporal; mustered out with the company
Solomon Alfred A. transferred to 97th N. Y. vols., June 8, 1864
Spencer William, discharged for disability
Stines Thomas, transferred to Artillery
Strubel Peter, transferred to 97th N. Y. vols., June 8, 1864
Snedeker John L. transferred to 97th N. Y. vols., June 8, 1864
Sutton Edward, discharged for disability

W.

Walsh James, killed at 1st. Fredericksburg
Wayte William, missing in action at Gettysburg
Wilson Matthew, discharged from wounds received at 2d. Bull Run
Wood Charles W. killed at South Mountain

DRUMMERS.

Hill William, promted Drum Major; mustered out with the company
Rollins Frank, mustered out with the company

RETURNED OFFICERS.

First Lieutenant, commanding.——Henry C. Barnum, formerly of company L.
Second Lieutenant.——Augustus P. Butler, formerly of comp. C

COMPANY I.*

ORIGINAL OFFICERS

Captain.——Peter J. Claassen, resigned
First Lieutenant.——George Wheaton, resigned
Second Lieutenant. ——Eno J. Claassen, promoted 1st. Lieutenant, Captain; ——

NON-COMMISSIONED OFFICERS.

SERGEANTS.

First.——Thomas Higgs, promoted 2d. Lieutenant; and 1st Lieutenant of company L.; mustered out with the regiment
Second.——George E. Allen, promoted 2d. Lieutenant; 1st. Lieutenant; discharged from wounds received at 1st. Fredericksburg

CORPORALS.

First.——Lester Lewis, discharged for disability
Second.——Benjamin F Bowne, promoted Sergeant; wounded at Antietam; wounded at Gettysburg; promoted 1st. Lieutenant; wounded at Spottsylvania; mustered out with the regiment
Third.——John Knipe, promoted Sergeant; killed at 1st. Fredericksburg
Fourth.——Thomas Hart, mustered out with the company
Fifth.——Arthur Blaney, wounded at Gettysburg; promoted Sergeant; 1st. Sergeant; mustered out with the company
Sixth.——William Black, wounded at Antietam; promoted Sergeant; re-enlisted; wounded at Laurel Hill: after the company was mustered out, remained with the 97th N. Y. vols.
Seventh.——Hynds James, promoted Sergeant; discharged from wounds received at Antietam

* This company left New York, July 20, 1861, and joined the regiment in the field, August 25, 1861. They were mustered out, August, 1864

PRIVATES.

B.

Beigle George, promoted Corporal; Sergeant; re-enlisted; after the company was mustered out, remained with the 97th N. Y. vols.
Bergen John, discharged from wounds received at 1st. Fredericksburg
Blair James, discharged from wounds received at 2d. Bull Run
Blythe James, wounded at 1st. Fredericksburg; ———
Bodenmiller George, promoted Corporal; killed at Spottsylvania
Boker Harvey, transferred to gun-boat service
Bowne Jeremiah H. discharged for disability
Brinkerhoff Walter, transferred to Veteran Reserve Corps
Brown John, wounded at 1st. Fredericksburg; transferred to Veteran Reserve Corps
Bullock John H. discharged for disability
Burke Michael, transferred to Signal Corps
Byrd John W. died of disease

C.

Casey John F. transferred to Veteran Reserve Corps
Chambers James, died of disease
Cole Benjamin, wounded at Antietam; ———
Coles George W. discharged for disability
Coles John H. discharged for disability
Curtin Daniel, killed at Antietam

D.

Demarest Charles, discharged for disability
Doremus David, transferred to Veteran Reserve Corps
Dumphry Michael, transferred to Signal Corps
Dyer John, discharged for disability

E.

Elliott Charles, discharged for disability

F.

Farrell Jesse W. discharged for disability
Ferry James, discharged for disability
Fitzgerald Absalom, promoted Corporal; taken prisoner at Spottsylvania, and died in the rebel prison at Andersonville, Georgia
Foley John, transferred to Veteran Reserve Corps

G.

Gibbons Frank P. promoted Corporal; mustered out with the company

H.

Hackett Michael, wounded at 1st. Fredericksburg; ———
Hartshorne Edward, discharged for disability
Hazeltine James, discharged for disability
Hicks Charles, mustered out with the company
Hicks George, promoted Corporal; wounded at Spottsylvania mustered out with the company
Hodgkiss Ebenezer, discharged from wounds received at Antietam
Hussey George, discharged by promotion

I.

Isaacs Isaac, discharged for disability

J.

Jarves Richard, mustered out with the company
Jones Samuel B. killed at 1st. Fredericksburg
Jordon John P. killed at 1st. Fredericksburg

K.

Kennedy Patrick, died from disease
Kinney Peter, died from wounds received at Antietam

L.

Lester Robert G. promoted Corporal; wounded in the Wilderness; mustered out with the company
Little Alexander, died of disease
Loughran John, discharged for disability

M.

Manley Hubert, wounded at 2d. Bull Run; promoted Corporal; wounded at Spottsylvania; mustered out with the company
Mathews Samuel, promoted Corporal; wounded in the Wilderness; mustered out with the company
McAvoy Joseph, killed at Antietam
McCanlis Thomas L. wounded at 2d. Bull Run; promoted Corporal; mustered out with the company
Moore John, discharged for disability
Morris Samuel, transferred to Artillery

O.

Owens James, discharged for disability

P.

Paul Stephen C. wounded at 1st. Fredericksburg; ———
Pettit James, discharged for disability

R.

Riker Robert L. killed at 2d. Bull Run.

S.

Schuberth George, promoted drummer; after the company was mustered out, remained with the 97th N. Y. vols.
Scott Walter, promoted Corporal; Sergeant; wounded at Spottsylvania; mustered out with the company
Sharrock Ralph, discharged for disability
Stewart Edward, wounded at Antietam; after the company was mustered out, remained with the 97th N. Y. vols.
Sweet Henry, discharged for disability

T.

Tabele Mathew L. promoted Corporal; Sergeant; mustered out with the company
Thompson William N. promoted Corporal; wounded in the Wilderness; mustered out with the company.
Tower Lucien N. killed at 1st. Fredericksburg
Trainor Joseph P. mustered out with the company

W.

Waterhouse Edward, missing at Bealton Station, Va., on the march
Westervelt Francis, killed at Gettysburg
Wolff Jacob, mustered out with the company

Y.

Youngman Theodore, taken prisoner at Gettysburg, exchanged; mustered out with the company

---

DRUMMER.

Keenan James, taken prisoner on the picket line, near Winchester, Va.

RETURNED OFFICER. *

First Lieutenant, commanding.——Benjamin F. Bowne, wounded

---

* This officer returned with the regiment, and was mustered out with it, June 23, 1864.

COMPANY L.*

ORIGINAL OFFICERS

Captain.——Erastus R. Miller, resigned
First Lieutenant.——A. Martin Burtis, appointed Quartermaster; mustered out with the company
Second Lieutenant.——Andrew B. Stiles, (see company D.)

NON-COMMISSIONED OFFICERS.
SERGEANTS.

First.——Samuel S. J. Briggs, (see company G.)
Second.——Henry J. Curry, promoted 1st. Sergeant; killed at Gettysburg
Third.——Henry V. Williamson (see company G.)

CORPORALS.

First.——John H. Scott, promoted Sergeant; killed at Antietam
Second.——Charles H. Townsend, promoted Sergeant; transferred to Veteran Reserve Corps
Third.——W. T. Wheeler, discharged for disability
Fourth.——C. E. Valentine, transferred to Veteran Reserve Corps
Fifth.——G. D. Carroll, discharged for disability
Sixth.——F. R. Ludlam, promoted Sergeant; Sergeant-Major; discharged by promotion
Seventh.——Astor Kissam, discharged for disability
Eighth.——Thomas Marcotte, promoted Sergeant; discharged by promotion

PRIVATES.
A.

Allen William E. killed in the Wilderness
Ames Charles M. mustered out with the company

---

*This company was mustered into service, August 31, 1861, and left New York city, September 12, 1861, to join the regiment in the field, where they arrived September 24, 1861. The company was mustered out, September, 1864.

B.

Bailey William S. killed at 1st. Fredericksburg
Bamberg Carl, wounded in the Wilderness; after the company was mustered out, remained with the 97th N. Y. vols.
Bamberg Maurice, wounded at Spottsylvania; after the company was mustered out, remained with the 97th N. Y. vols.
Bancroft Charles W. discharged by promotion
Barnum Henry C. promoted Corporal; Sergeant; 1st. Sergeant; 2d. Lieutenant of company H; also 1st. Lieutenant and Captain of company H; mustered out with that company
Becker William, discharged for disability
Bell John H. killed at 1st. Fredericksburg
Blayney George, mustered out with the company
Bouquinn Lawrence H. wounded at Chancellorsville; promoted Sergeant-Major; mustered out with the company
Brophy Patrick, mustered out with the company
Brown John H. promoted Corporal; mustered out with the company
Brown Samuel, transferred to Veteran Reserve Corps
Brown Thomas, promoted Corporal; died of disease
Bunte George, promoted Corporal; killed in the Wilderness
Burns Thomas, re-enlisted; after the company was mustered out, remained with the 97th N. Y. vols.

C.

Callan Patrick, re-enlisted; after the company was mustered out, remained with the 97th N. Y. vols.
Carter James B. promoted Corporal; wounded at 1st. Fredericksburg; transferred to Veteran Reserve Corps
Chappel Clark, promoted Corporal; wounded in the Wilderness; after the company was mustered out, remained with the 97th N. Y. vols.
Clark John, killed at Spottsylvania
Cochrane John, discharged by promotion
Connor Charles, killed at 1st. Fredericksburg
Craig William, killed at 1st. Fredericksburg
Crawford E. discharged for disability
Cross Charles J. killed at Antietam
Curtis William, discharged for disability

D.

Dailey Frederick, discharged by promotion
Danburg William, discharged from wounds received at 1st. Fredericksburg
Davis Robert H. mustered out with the company
De Vere Samuel, mustered out with the Company

De Voe Edwin F. mustered out with the company
Douglass Benjamin F. promoted Corporal; Sergeant; killed at Spottsylvania

E.
Eagan Daniel, promoted Corporal; mustered out with the company;

F.
Folger Robert H. mustered out with the company

G.
Graham James A. transferred to Artillery
Graham William A. mustered out with the company

H.
Hatterick Samuel, discharged for disability
Hendershott Joseph, wounded in the Wilderness; mustered out with the company
Hodson Edward, discharged for disability
Holt Frederick, discharged for disability
Hosey Patrick, promoted Corporal; wounded in the Wilderness; mustered out with the company

I.
Imlay John K. mustered out with the company

J.
Jenkins William A. taken prisoner at 1st. Fredericksburg, exchanged; taken prisoner in the Wilderness, exchanged; after the company was mustered out, remained with the 97th N. Y. vols.
Johnson John J. promoted Corporal; Sergeant; wounded at 1st. Fredericksburg; discharged from wounds received at Spottsylvania

K.
Keating Thomas, mustered out with the company
Kelley Henry J. promoted Corporal; wounded in the Wilderness; mustered out with the company
Kelley John J. promoted Corporal; Sergeant; re-enlisted; after the company was mustered out, remained with the 97th N. Y. vols.
Kerr Thomas, died from wounds received at Spottsylvania

L.
Lewis Warren J. discharged by promotion
Lober Jacob, killed in the Wilderness
Lockington John S. re-enlisted; after the company was mustered out, remained with the 97th N. Y. vols.

M.

Malone John, promoted Corporal; wounded at 1st. Fredericksburg; mustered out with the company
Mantle George, transferred to Artillery
Marran Patrick, wounded at Antietam; re-enlisted; after the company was mustered out, remained with the 97th N. Y. vols.
Marsellus Joseph V. promoted Corporal; Sergeant; discharged from wounds received at Spottsylvania
Martin James, discharged from wounds received at Antietam
McDonald Martin discharged for disability
Mead Augustus W. promoted Corporal; wounded in the Wilderness; after the company was mustered out, remained with the 97th N. Y. vols.
Melville James C. discharged for disability
Meyer Albert B. died of disease
Montey Benjamin J. killed at Spottsylvania
Murphy John, discharged for disability
Murray Mark A. wounded at 1st. Fredericksburg; mustered out with the company

O.

Osborne Jeremiah, killed at 1st. Fredericksburg

P.

Platt George C. taken prisoner at Gettysburg, exchanged; mustered out with the company

R.

Roberts Thomas, discharged for disability

S.

Simpson John, discharged from wounds received at Antietam
Skinner Charles, killed at 1st. Fredericksburg
Southworth Chester, discharged by promotion
Supple John, mustered out with the company

T.

Thompson Henry G. discharged for disability
Thompson James, mustered out with the company
Thoms Edwin, mustered out with the company

V.

Van Alst John I. jr. promoted Corporal; Sergeant; Sergeant-Major; 1st. Lieutenant; Captain; wounded at Spottsylvania; mustered out with the regiment
Van Cleef Joseph V. wounded at Antietam; transferred to regular army

Van Norden Samuel G. promoted Corporal; Sergeant; 1st. Sergeant; wounded at Antietam; taken prisoner in the Wilderness, exchanged; mustered out with the company
Voshage Adolph, discharged from wounds received at Antietam

W.

Watson Samuel S. transferred to gun-boat service
Whaites Charles, discharged from wounds received at 2d. Bull Run
Willers John A. promoted Corporal; killed at Antietam
Willet John C. discharged for disability
Willis John, deserted on the battle-field of Cedar Mountain
Wilsey Charles, discharged for disability
Wilsey Harvey B. discharged for diisability
Wood Emanuel L. mustered out with the company

RETURNED OFFICERS.*

Captain.——John I. Van Alst, jr. wounded
First Lieutenant.——Thomas Higgs, formerly of company L

RETURNED REGIMENTAL OFFICERS.

Colonel.——Joseph A. Moesch, formerly of company B., killed
Lieutenant Colonel.——William H. Chalmers, came from home and joined the regiment in October, 1863
Major.——Henry V. Williamson, formerly of company G.
Adjutant.——Henry P. Claire, formerly of company D.
Quartermaster.——A. Martin Burtis, formerly of company L.
Surgeon.——Charles J. Nordquiest
Assistant Surgeon.——A. V. Ketcham, joined the regiment in the winter of 1862, and was transferred to another regiment, June 8, 1864
Chaplain.——A. Roe, came from home and joined the regiment, in the winter of 1863, and was transferred to another regiment, June 8, 1864

☞ Mr. NEYER, and his band, joined the regiment in the Field, in June, 1861, and was mustered out by an order from the War Department, July, 1862

*These officers were mustered out with the regiment, June 23, 1864, in New York city.

TABLE A.

Showing a complete List of those who were Killed, or Died from wounds received in battle.

	A	B	C	D	E	F	G	H	I	L	Total
Harpers Ferry, Md.	1						1				2
Cedar Mountain, Va.		1									1
Second Bull Run, Va.	5			5	1	1	2		1		15
South Mountain, Md.								1			1
Antietam, Md.	3	4		2			4	3	3	2	21
First Fredericksburg, Va.	4	7	3	3	5	1	1	1	4	6	35
Gettysburg, Pa.		1	2				1	1	1	1	7
Wilderness, Va.	3	3	2		1	4			3	3	16
Laurel Hill, Va.	1						1				2
Spottsylvania, Va.									4	1	5
Total,											105

TABLE B.

Showing a complete List of those who were wounded in battle.

	A	B	C	D	E	F	G	H	I	L	Total
Harpers Ferry, Va.			1				1				2
Second Bull Run, Va.	1			1	2	1	4	1	3	1	14
Antietam, Md.	3	2	9	12	8	10	13	2	6	6	71
First Fredericksburg, Va.	5	10	13	10	5	12	5	6	6	4	76
Chancellorsville, Va.									1		1
Gettysburg, Pa.			2	1		4	1		2		10
Wilderness, Va.	4	6	2	2	3	2	5	4	3	6	37
Laurel Hill, Va.	5										5
Spottsylvania, Va.	2				1			1	4	4	12
Coal Harbor, Va.	1										1
Total,											229

www.ingramcontent.com/pod-product-compliance
Lightning Source LLC
Chambersburg PA
CBHW031736230426
43669CB00007B/361